BRAND IT LIKE
SERHANT

Also by Ryan Serhant

*Sell It Like Serhant: How to Sell More, Earn More, and
Become the Ultimate Sales Machine
Big Money Energy: How to Rule at Work,
Dominate at Life, and Make Millions*

BRAND IT LIKE
SERHANT

STAND OUT FROM THE CROWD, BUILD YOUR FOLLOWING, AND EARN MORE MONEY

by RYAN SERHANT

Go

hachette
BOOKS

NEW YORK

Hachette Go, an imprint of Hachette Books
Hachette Book Group
1290 Avenue of the Americas
New York, NY 10104
HachetteGo.com
Facebook.com/HachetteGo
Instagram.com/HachetteGo

First Edition: January 2024

Published by Hachette Go, an imprint of Hachette Book Group, Inc.
The Hachette Go name and logo are trademarks of the Hachette Book Group.

The Hachette Speakers Bureau provides a wide range of authors for speaking events. To find out more, visit hachettespeakersbureau.com or email HachetteSpeakers@hbgusa.com.

Hachette Go books may be purchased in bulk for business, educational, or promotional use. For information, please contact your local bookseller or email the Hachette Book Group Special Markets Department at Special.Markets@hbgusa.com.

The publisher is not responsible for websites (or their content) that are not owned by the publisher.

Library of Congress Cataloging-in-Publication Data

Name: Serhant, Ryan, author.
Title: Brand it like Serhant: stand out from the crowd, build your
    following, and earn more money / by Ryan Serhant.
Description: First edition. | New York, NY: Hachette Go, 2024.
Identifiers: LCCN 2023037542 | ISBN 9780306923128 (hardcover) | ISBN
    9780306923135 (trade paperback) | ISBN 9780306923142 (ebook)
Subjects: LCSH: Branding (Marketing) | Marketing—Management.
Classification: LCC HF5415.1255 .S47 2024 | DDC 658.8/27—dc23/eng/20230814
LC record available at https://lccn.loc.gov/2023037542

ISBNs: 978-0-306-92312-8 (hardcover); 978-0-306-92314-2 (ebook);
978-0-306-83548-3 (signed edition)

Printed in the United States of America

LSC-H

Printing 1, 2023

This book is dedicated to my mom, the woman who taught me—along with everything else I know—that your first impression will be your last impression if you're not careful. Mom, as proof that I listen to you and respect your opinion, there's less swearing in this book than my first two.

Contents

CONTENTS

BRAND IT LIKE
SERHANT

Introduction:
Build a Brand on a
Solid Foundation

One of the craziest days of my life as a luxury real estate broker started off like any other day. I was up extra early to get a jump start on answering emails. I did my workout. It was legs day, and that's *the worst*. By 7:00 a.m. I was suited up, in the car, and headed to the office. I had looked at my calendar the night before, so I knew my schedule was packed. On the way to Manhattan, my phone was already blowing up with texts and emails. By the time I got to the office, it was nonstop. There were meetings with developers, meetings with clients, calls from excited buyers, and texts from nervous sellers, and we shot a video on the roof deck of a new building we would be selling in Tribeca. The views were insane!

My last meeting of the day was a long brainstorming session/planning meeting. The previous year, I had decided to take a huge step forward and launch my own company. Starting a new business felt like a never-ending game of Whac-A-Mole. We'd knock something off the enormous to-do list only to have it immediately

1

replaced by another task. We had to find the right office space. (Where should it be? How much space would we need? And wait, *all this is going to cost how much?*) We needed a great name and a new logo. The website would need to be completely rehauled. We'd hire more team members, buy just the right furniture, find a CFO, create a team to develop our classes and mentoring program, file tons of paperwork, buy lots of Twizzlers, and write a business plan. It was overwhelming at times, but I was excited about all of it. I was used to hard work, I had a great team, and I had connections, experience, and a good reputation in the industry. THIS WILL BE GREAT! is what I thought most of the time. I couldn't ignore the fact that there was so much uncertainty in the world, much of it due to COVID, and this planted a pesky seed of doubt in my mind. *Why am I starting a huge business in the middle of a pandemic? Who does that? What if everyone decides to leave this densely packed city for somewhere safer . . . like the moon? I can't sell apartments in a city that has a population of zero!* I'd glance down at my hands, wondering if I could rekindle my hand modeling work if worse came to worst. When I really needed reassurance, I reminded myself of my favorite quote: "Take care of the work, and the work will take care of you." This has always been a mantra of mine, and it has served me well. I'd take a breath and just focus on the task (albeit an enormous one) in front of me.

We wrapped up the meeting and all stepped away with long to-do lists. READY, SET, GO, EVERYONE! The day had flown by in a flash. I answered a few more emails and texts and walked outside to meet Yuriy, my driver and longtime friend, and drive back to Brooklyn. It was a late August evening, and I noticed the air felt heavy. Hurricane Ida had landed in New Orleans a couple of days earlier, and the tail end of that storm was headed our way in the form of heavy rain. The traffic was surprisingly light, and I got home quickly. I said good night to Yuriy and walked into my dark and completely silent house. My wife is from Greece, and my family spends the summer there, so the usual sounds of toddler feet and Emilia chatting with her mother in her native language were missing. While they were away, I worked extra late and came home to an empty house every night and ate dinner alone while streaming TV shows like a sad bachelor. I microwaved my food and sat down to finish the latest season of *Succession*. Halfway through the first episode, it started to rain. By the time that episode was over, it sounded like I was living directly underneath Niagara Falls. *Whoa, this rain is bananas.* I looked out the front window and was surprised to see that our street, the one we drove on and walked on every single day, had vanished. In its place was a class five rapid . . . in Brooklyn!

As I looked at the raging river from the safety of our parlor-level floor, I thought about how grateful I was that our house was safe and sturdy. Thanks to my connections in real estate, I had access to the best architects and contractors. Our brand-new six-story, 8,000-square-foot house that we had just moved into had been built to last and was very safe. In addition to the twenty-seven steel beams we added to the structure to make the house extra strong, we installed a sprinkler system and a security system that could rival those of the White House. We also got a permit to widen the garden floor doorway so no one would break their neck getting Zena's stroller in and out. Finally, we had the house blessed by a Greek Orthodox priest who doused the entire place in holy water. We were fully protected when it came to fire, stroller mishaps, bands of robbers, and demons. Surely the house could handle the rain, right?

As soon as this thought passed through my head, the rain that was already pounding down got even louder. A terrifying roaring noise seemed to be coming from the back of the house. I walked into the kitchen and looked out the window. *Oh. There's a lake in our backyard, and it's rising right before my eyes. This can't be good.* I was starting to get nervous. Really, really nervous. We had spent four years renovating the house! Was I going to have to call Emilia before she came home? *Puffer, I can't wait for you to get back, but quick heads up. Soooooo. It rained really hard, and our new house broke free from its foundation, and it sailed down the street like a cruise ship headed for the Caribbean. Now we're going to live in a hotel! Also, the entire family will need all new clothes/shoes/everything. Okay-see-you-at-the-airport-love-you-bye!*

This was Noah's Ark–level rain, and it did not stop. I decided I had to face the music and see if any of this water was coming into the lower floors of the house. I crept down the stairs cautiously, like a character in a horror film who knows he's about to die at the hands of a deranged killer. What I saw was more terrifying than Freddy Krueger himself. There was water EVERYWHERE. It was pouring in fast and rising quickly and destroying everything in its path. *Oh shit!* I grabbed the first object I saw, which happened to be a broom. Picture me, in my favorite Lululemon workout shorts, frantically trying to push hundreds of gallons of rushing water out of my house with a broom. I'm sure Mother Nature herself was laughing, pointing out the absurdity of the situation to all her earthy friends. *Oh my God. Do you see the guy with the broom? Hilarious, right? Doesn't he know I can take out entire neighborhoods with one breath if I feel like it? Silly humans!*

I didn't know what to do. While there have been times in my life when I wasn't 100 percent sure of the right course of action, I have prided myself on being able to figure things out. I have never felt as helpless as I did on that day, and it was scary. I stood there frozen, on the verge of tears, knowing the reality was I couldn't do anything to keep the water outside where it belonged. I tried to call Emilia, but with the time difference in Greece I couldn't reach her (not that she could do anything other than listen to me cry).

Assuming I wasn't the only one with an ocean inside of their home, I called the neighbors on each side of us to make sure they were okay. "Hi, wow. It's Ryan. I can't believe how much water is in my house! I just wanted to see if you're okay! Do you have lots of damage?" Both sets of neighbors had the same general response: "We're totally fine, just hanging out and watching TV and eating snacks, and no, we're not having any problems with water at all." After hanging up the phone I felt even worse. *Seriously? It's just us? So, the houses that are over a century old can handle this no problem? But our brand-new house is apparently as waterproof as a cardboard box?* Feeling more desperate and scared, I called 911. They told me to get to higher ground . . . that was it. I was alone, with nothing but a broom, watching all our hopes and dreams float away. *Goodbye, ultra-comfortable screening room. Goodbye, mother-in-law suite. So long, home gym of my dreams. It was nice knowing you for a few weeks.*

Ida did a lot of damage to our house, but I know we got off lucky. The storm brought unprecedented rainfall, and the flooding paralyzed New York City. The subways filled with water, cars floated away, and property was destroyed all over the tristate area—but it got much worse. Dozens of people lost their lives that day. In the end, I was just grateful to be safe and unharmed.

Fast-forward to Emilia and me meeting with engineers, architects, and contractors about getting the house back in order. The bottom line? It turned out our foundation SUCKED. We had done all our renovations on a foundation that did not provide enough support. Without going into lots of boring detail, if we didn't get a new foundation, we could look forward to more problems from surprise floods, tornadoes, hurricanes, high winds, blizzards, alien invasions, zombie apocalypses, robot uprisings, and plagues of locusts. This was a *very* expensive fix. It was also going to take up so much time that I considered giving up and moving us all into a tent. In a million years I could never have imagined a rainy day could cause so much damage. Then there were the countless items we needed to replace. Between the new business and our house, I felt like I'd spend the rest of my life just shopping. Who has time for that?

I started listing things off to Emilia. "Oh my God. We need new floors, chairs, tables, and a sofa and . . ."

She cut me off. "Ryan. Our house flooded, but it's going to be okay. The stuff doesn't matter right now. It is our family that matters, not the stuff inside of our house. This is the place we built to make memories and live our lives together no matter what happens. It will be a mess for a while. So what? It's not like the flood crushed our hopes and plans for our family." I must have looked skeptical (I really liked our sofa), because Emilia looked just a little annoyed with me. "Ryan, it's going to be fine. We know exactly what the problem is. We need to focus on fixing our foundation. The foundation is our priority. Then I promise we'll find a new sofa you'll like, okay?"

Suddenly, my anxiety about all the stuff I needed for the house and the new company started to seem like a waste of energy. I had been swimming around in such an enormous sea of practical details about building the new company that I forgot that when it comes to my business, I know what I'm doing! I'm an excellent salesperson. I have enough experience and the right contacts. I'm a solid negotiator. I've proven to myself over and over again that I can manage the most difficult situations and challenging clients. I've gone above and beyond to get deals done: throw a party for babies, deliver sweet potato fries to a client in the middle of the night . . . and I bet I'm the only broker who has been kidnapped in a foreign country and still made it to a closing on time. There was no doubt that I had all the basics down, but I needed something big and strong to support everything I wanted to accomplish with my new company. It clicked for me that if my foundation wasn't rock-solid, it didn't matter where my office was or what kind of suits I wore, I'd just be a guy who is good at selling real estate. I understood that if I wanted my business to thrive and stand strong, I had to focus my energy on what would be the *heart and soul* of the company. I needed to build a brand that was bigger, better, and stronger than anything I had built before. I needed to build a brand that would take me into the future.

YOUR BRAND IS YOUR FOUNDATION

To be clear, this was NOT the first time I had thought about my brand. I have been aware of the power of personal brands since the early days when I was the "gray-haired broker on that reality TV show." I had a website and a big social media presence; I was on a hit television show; I had a solid reputation as a successful broker; and I had a driver, classy business cards, and an office in SoHo. That was all great! But now I wanted to maximize the power of my brand and use it for all it was worth. I wanted a brand so powerful that it brought in business *while I was sleeping.* What followed was an exciting period of examination. I wanted to dig deep and examine my values, what I stood for, what my purpose was. While every brand has a visual identity (and that's important), I didn't want to jump into names, colors, logos, and fonts until I uncovered the essence of the company I was building. Otherwise, what's the point? I thought long and hard about the image I wanted to project to the world. I developed a clear vision of how I would use media to create an entirely new way of selling. I reflected on who I was at my core and what unique qualities about myself and my company we should showcase. The question was, how do I wrap all those ideas into a package that consistently makes it clear that SERHANT.* is the go-to brokerage for buying and selling luxury properties all over the world?

In addition to all that contemplation, I spent countless hours with my team designing a system to establish, grow, and maintain the foundation of our company—our brand, SERHANT. Eventually we came up with our very own Brand Strategy System, and it's become our in-house bible of branding. Our three-part system accomplishes a few key things: how to find and establish a core identity, how to create and use consistent content to generate brand awareness, and how to strategically develop a plan for sharing wins by "shouting it from the mountaintop." This is the exact same system we used to develop SERHANT., now the most followed real estate brand in the world. The system *works*. This

---

* In case you were wondering, the ALL CAPS and the period at the end of my name are intentional and serve an important purpose. We'll get to logos a little later.

isn't a throw-everything-on-a-vision-board-and-see-what-pops-to-life approach. The system is structured and insightful, and if you stick with me throughout the following chapters, you will uncover the unique brand that exists inside of you. You'll learn how to use your personal brand to gain visibility, attract higher-quality clients, earn more money, and exceed every expectation you've set for yourself. If you've already started building your brand, this system will help you take it to a higher level so you can earn more. Together we'll home in on your strengths and maximize your brand's power, so you'll have clients flocking to you in droves, sending your business and income through the roof.

After my new house nearly washed away, I realized that we can never predict what the universe has in store for us. We have to be ready to accept whatever it is—slow housing markets, inflation, ice storms, killer bees, vampires, supply chain issues, recessions, etc.—and move forward the best we can. This is why crafting a personal brand is so important when it comes to protecting your livelihood. A brand isn't just a building, a store, a website, or a person—it's something much bigger. When you build a brand, you're making a vow to uphold the values at the core of that brand. You're making a promise to your customers that you'll always create the best possible experience for them. Those values and promises are something that can never be taken from you, not even during a hundred-year flood.

To borrow a thought from Dr. George Berkeley, the philosopher and Anglican bishop from the 1600s, "If a tree falls in the forest and no one is around to hear it, does it make a sound?" If someone is the best graphic designer, dog walker, yoga instructor, real estate broker, professional organizer, or personal chef *and no one knows about it, does it matter*? The branding system I'm going to share in this book is about making what you do *matter*. The foundation my team and I built is strong enough to support all of us, and I know it will hold up as we continue to grow. The SERHANT. Brand Strategy System helped me build my brand from the ground up, and now I've made it my mission in life to help YOU unleash the brand that lives inside of you.

My hands-on experience of building a brand one step at a time puts me in a perfect position to help you discover your brand so you can use it to increase your business. Since focusing heavily on my brand, my company has expanded into six more states; I've closed record-breaking deals, landed *the most expensive* listing in the entire country, started filming a new TV show, written books (*Sell It Like Serhant: How to Sell More, Earn More, and Become the Ultimate Sales Machine*; *Big Money Energy: How to Rule at Work, Dominate at Life, and Make Millions*; and now this one!), and sold billions of dollars' worth of real estate. The huge jump in my business is why I am WILDLY EXCITED to share this system with you. I know you can do this, and I can't wait to get started. (I'm practically jumping out of my chair while I write this!)

Before we start working together, I want you to know that my approach is unique, and no other book provides the guidance and expertise I'm going to give you. Together we will tap into your core identity, discover your brand's true personality, and talk about best social media practices and how to establish credibility. We'll grow your audience into a community, develop the right visual identity, and create an efficient content calendar to make it all manageable. All these steps (and many more) are going to pull that brand out of you so you can transform it into a powerhouse of a business. Whether you're an entrepreneur, a gig worker, working at an established company, pivoting jobs, starting your dream company, or a ten-year-old kid who wants to disrupt the current model of lemonade stands, this book is the bible that will show you exactly how successful you can be when YOU take control of your brand.

I'm not leaving this all up to me. I've called in some reinforcements. As part of my quest to help you build the best personal brand possible, I sat down and interviewed the people behind some of the most successful personal brands around. I've talked to brands all over the spectrum too—fashion brands, chefs, influencers, best-selling authors, gamers, designers, and entrepreneurs whose brands have become household names—to get their take on building a personal brand. Now it's your turn to get started on your branding journey.

So, let's do this. I'm going to show you how to take full control of the brand inside of you. Then you're going to build a strong foundation for your business that can handle all your future growth, and finally you're going to watch your business crush even your craziest and most outrageous vision for success. Got it?

READY, SET, GO!

MEET THE BRANDS

Tom Bilyeu

Tom Bilyeu is the cofounder of the brand Quest Nutrition, which was acquired by Simply Good Foods for $1 billion in 2019. Tom is also the cofounder and host of *Impact Theory*, a company devoted to helping people develop the skills they need to improve themselves and the world. *Impact Theory*'s content and Tom's public speaking "inspire people to unlock their potential and pursue greatness." Tom was named one of *Success* magazine's Top 25 Influential People in 2018 and Entrepreneur of the Year by Secret Entourage in 2016.

Justina Blakeney

Justina Blakeney is an interdisciplinary artist, designer, and best-selling author. She is the founder and creative director of home decor brand Jungalow and the author of several design books, including *Jungalow: Decorate Wild*, *The New Bohemians Handbook: Come Home to Good Vibes*, and the *New York Times* bestseller *The New Bohemians: Cool and Collected Homes*. Justina's design collections are sold online at Jungalow.com, and her newest collection, Opalhouse Designed with Jungalow, is available at Target and at Target.com. Justina was featured on the cover of *Architectural Digest* in June 2022. Her work has also been featured in *House Beautiful*; *Entrepreneur*; *Coastal Living*; *Domino*; *Martha Stewart Living*; *O, The Oprah Magazine*; *Essence*; and *Good Housekeeping*, among others.

Neil Brown

Neil Brown is the cofounder with his late wife, Amsale Aberra, of Amsale, one of the world's leading luxury bridal houses. The company was inspired by Amsale's quest to find a wedding dress with a modern silhouette for her own wedding during a time when ornate gowns were the trend. Amsale's dresses have been featured on *Grey's Anatomy*, *American Wedding*, *27 Dresses*, *The Hangover*, *The View*, and the *Oprah Winfrey Show*. Notable women have worn her dresses, including Halle Berry, Julia Roberts, Salma Hayek, Lucy Liu, Vivica A. Fox, Heather Graham, Lisa Kudrow, Katherine Heigl, Heidi Klum, and Hilaria Baldwin.

Athena Calderone

Athena Calderone, founder of the lifestyle brand EyeSwoon, is a creative director, author, interior designer, chef, and entertaining expert. Athena recently launched a furniture and tabletop collection with Crate & Barrel and a line of rugs with Beni. She is the best-selling author of the design book *Live Beautiful*, and her cookbook, *Cook Beautiful*, received a James Beard award. Athena has been featured in *Vogue*, *Architectural Digest*, *New York Times*, *Wall Street Journal*, *Vanity Fair*, *Harper's Bazaar*, *InStyle*, *Elle Decor*, and *New York Magazine*, and she is a recurring guest on the *Today* show.

Kenneth Cole

Kenneth Cole is a designer and social activist who founded the billion-dollar global brand Kenneth Cole Productions in

1982. Kenneth's designs are modern and versatile, and his collections include clothing, shoes, accessories, fragrances, watches, jewelry, and eyewear, which are sold in over ninety retail locations. Kenneth believes business and philanthropy are interdependent, and he launched the first public service campaign for AIDS in 1985. He has served on amFAR's board of directors, eventually becoming chair, and has recently launched the Mental Health Coalition to end the stigma against mental health conditions.

Sebastian Diamond

Sebastian Diamond, a.k.a. FaZe CBass, is the cofounder of FaZe Clan, the prominent and influential e-gaming organization that was created when he was still in high school. FaZe Clan has a global fan base of over 510 million and offers video blogs, lifestyle and branded content, gaming highlights, and live streams of gaming tournaments. FaZe Clan's roster of influential personalities consists of content creators, e-sports professionals, and world-class gamers, as well as NFL star Kyler "FaZe K1" Murray; Lebron "FaZe Bronny" James Jr.; Lil Yachty, a.k.a. "FaZe Boat"; and Snoop Dogg, a.k.a. "FaZe Snoop." FaZe Clan has collaborated with Porsche, Nissan, Nike, DoorDash, McDonald's, Xfinity, and Totino's. FaZe Clan went public in 2022 with a valuation of $725 million.

Mike Evans

Mike Evans is the founder of Fixer and a cofounder of Grub-Hub. Fixer is a "right now" handyman service that allows people to book "fixers" for home maintenance, including plumbing, electrical work, painting and drywall, and furniture assembly. Mike's first business, GrubHub, was born when he wanted to order a late-night pizza and discovered there were no easy options available for doing so. Twelve years after that pizza craving, GrubHub merged with Seamless and was valued at $2.04 billion. After the IPO, Mike left GrubHub and rode his bike 4,200 miles along the TransAm bike path from Virginia to California. Mike is also the author of the business memoir *Hangry: A Startup Journey*.

Iman Gadzhi

Iman Gadzhi dropped out of high school at the age of seventeen and accidentally started a business that would grow into IAG Media, an e-commerce marketing agency that helps businesses scale through the use of paid traffic and sales funnels. As a teenager, Iman first offered social media management to a local football team. After succeeding with that endeavor, Iman's passion and talent for content creation resulted in enough referrals to launch his own company. After just two and a half years, Iman was earning $100,000 a month. Now Iman owns several businesses, including AgenciFlow, a leading software company, and Gents Croquet Club, one of the best-performing NFT projects.

Ryan Holiday

Ryan Holiday is a writer and media strategist who had a successful marketing career at American Apparel after dropping out of college at the age of nineteen. He is the founder of the creative agency Brass Check, which has advised clients like Google, TASER, Complex, and best-selling authors Neil Strauss, Tony Robbins, and Tim Ferris. He is also the author of several best-selling books, including *The Obstacle Is the Way*, *Ego Is the Enemy*, *The Daily Stoic*, *Conspiracy*, and *Stillness Is the Key*, which have sold more than two million copies and have been published in thirty languages.

Mark Manson

Mark Manson is the author of the number one *New York Times* bestseller *The Subtle Art of Not Giving a F*ck: A Counterintuitive Approach to Living a Good Life* and *Everything Is F*cked: A Book About Hope* and is the coauthor with Will Smith of his memoir, *Will*. Mark's books have sold nearly twenty million copies worldwide and have been translated into more than sixty-five languages. Mark has also been published and featured in the *New York Times Magazine*, *GQ*, the *Guardian*, the BBC, *Time* magazine, the *New York Times*, *USA Today*, the *New York Post*, Buzzfeed, *Vice*, *Variety*, and others.

Rebecca Minkoff

Rebecca Minkoff is the founder of the eponymous global brand that is an industry leader in accessible luxury, handbags, accessories, and apparel. Her designs are known for blending femininity with a rock 'n' roll edge, and her Morning After Bag is considered a fashion icon. Her designs are sold at high-end retailers, including Nordstrom, Bloomingdale's, and Saks Fifth Avenue. Rebecca also established the Female Founder Collective, a network to empower woman-owned businesses. In 2022, her brand was acquired by Sunrise Brands, a diversified apparel company.

Daniella Monet

Daniella Monet is an entrepreneur and actress best known for her role as Trina Vega in the hit Nickelodeon show *Victorious*. Daniella stopped eating meat when she was just five years old and adopted a plant-based lifestyle as a teenager. She is the cofounder of Kinder Beauty, a vegan beauty box subscription service, and Daniella's Digest, a paid membership app designed to help people live their best lives by following a plant-based lifestyle.

Lewis Morgan

Lewis Morgan is the cofounder of Gymshark, an athleisure brand he started with a friend when he was still in college. Gymshark grew into a global brand that has been valued at $1.45 billion. He is currently the executive chair of AYBL Group, a brand of women's activewear and athleisure wear.

Carla Lalli Music

Carla Lalli Music is a chef, cookbook author, and YouTube personality. She was editor-at-large of *Bon Appétit* magazine. She was also the host of the popular cooking show *Back-to-Back Chef* on *Bon Appétit*'s YouTube channel, which featured guests such as Natalie Portman, Elizabeth Olsen,

BRAND IT LIKE SERHANT

Ellie Kemper, Michael Shannon, Marlon Wayans, and Al Roker, among many others. Carla is also the author of the cookbooks *Where Cooking Begins* and *That Sounds So Good*.

Nate O'Brien

Nate O'Brien started his first YouTube channel from his college dorm room at Penn State University with the mission of helping people live their best lives by focusing on the inner workings of finance, productivity, and personal development. Today, his YouTube channel has amassed over 1.1 million subscribers and 50 million views. Nate has been featured in *Forbes* and *Women's Wear Daily* and on CNBC.

Nadya Okamoto

Nadya Okamoto is the cofounder of August, a lifestyle brand working to reimagine periods and redefine the period experience. She is also the founder of PERIOD (period.org), an organization fighting to end period poverty and stigma. Nadya is the author of *Period Power: A Manifesto for the Menstrual Movement*. She has been recognized on the *Forbes* 30 Under 30 list, the Bloomberg 50 "Ones to Watch," and *People* magazine's Women Changing the World. Her work has also been featured in CNN, *Forbes*, the *Washington Post*, *The Cut*, the *New York Times*, *Good Morning America*, the *Today* show, *People*, *Teen Vogue*, NBC News, *Allure*, *Refinery 29*, *Vox*, *Bustle*, *Self*, *InStyle*, *Elle*, NBC News, the BBC, *Huffpost*, *Cosmopolitan*, *Harper's Bazaar*, the *Daily Mail*, and others.

Alison Roman

Alison Roman is a cook, writer, and author of three cookbooks—the *New York Times* bestseller *Nothing Fancy* as well as *Dining In* and *Sweet Enough*—and produces her own YouTube channel, Home Movies. Alison is known for her candor and wit; her recipes have become viral classics simply known as "the cookie," "the stew," and "the dip."

Nik Sharma

Nik Sharma is the CEO of Sharma Brands, a strategic initiatives firm working with a wide range of brands to help grow and scale revenue across digital platforms. Nik is one of *AdWeek*'s Young & Influential, *Forbes*'s 30 Under 30, *Business Insider*'s up-and-coming Investors to Watch, and an investor and adviser to some of the fastest-growing brands in commerce.

Griffin Thall

Griffin Thall is the CEO and cofounder of Pura Vida Bracelets, the multimillion-dollar jewelry and lifestyle brand. Griffin is responsible for growing the brand via digital marketing, social media, and influencer marketing. As a result, Pura Vida has nearly two million Instagram followers, making it the most-engaged jewelry brand on the platform. Griffin was included on the *Forbes* 30 Under 30 list in 2015, and Pura Vida has landed on *Inc.*'s list of the 5,000 Fastest-Growing Private Companies in America. Pura Vida was also named *LA Business Journal*'s DTC Brand of the Year. In 2019, Griffin was integral in helping the brand secure a $130 million investment from the iconic lifestyle brand Vera Bradley.

Mona Vand

Mona Vand is a trained pharmacist who uses her education and work experience to share health information in a relatable and digestible way. An expert in nutrition and natural wellness, her mission is to help keep people off of medications in the first place. Mona has been featured on *The Doctors*, NBC, Page Six, *Access Hollywood*, the *Telegraph*, Yahoo Finance, and more.

Gary Vaynerchuk

Gary Vaynerchuk, known as Gary Vee, is an entrepreneur, cofounder of the restaurant reservation software company Resy and Empathy Wines, and the author of four *New York Times* best-selling books. Gary is also the cofounder of VaynerMedia, an agency focusing on strategy, full-service creative, influencer marketing, e-commerce, personal branding, SMB marketing, and in-house consulting. Gary has more than forty-four million combined followers across his social media platforms, and his podcast *The GaryVee Audio Experience* is a global top 100 business podcast.

CASE STUDY: BRAND BUILDING IN ACTION

I'm also very excited to introduce you to Sydney Sherman. Sydney isn't just building a brand for herself; she's also the head of client relationship strategies at SERHANT. Sydney has graciously agreed to give us all an inside look as she builds her brand, Self by Syd, using the SERHANT. Brand Strategy System. At the end of each chapter, Sydney is going to share the results from her exercises (the same ones you'll be doing) as well as any thoughts, struggles, or successes she encounters along the way.

I'm Sydney, a twenty-eight-year-old New York City transplant from Binghamton, New York. After graduating out of competitive dance and starting my collegiate journey, I realized quickly how challenging it is to stay active, healthy, and happy when you have no one guiding you. I put myself through endless programs from my favorite influencers, counted every calorie I consumed, read every self-help book on the shelf, and still, I was tired, achy, and sad.

In 2021, I started taking my health into my own hands and thus, Self by Syd was born. Instagram influencers are loud, scientific journals are confusing, and personal trainers aren't accessible for everyone. I'm here to challenge the industry as we know it—and I'm here for you.

My goal is to be your guide and help you cut out the noise, tune inward, and learn to optimize a wellness routine for your best self.

Self by Syd is my passion project, because as you just learned, I am lucky to also spend my days building client relationship strategies at SERHANT., and I help educate the brand builders of tomorrow at Binghamton University (go Bearcats!).

Selfbysyd.com

CHAPTER 1

The New Road to Success Is Paved with Good Branding

Your brand is the heart and soul of your company. It is also the bright light that will guide you through the entirely new and unprecedented work environment we've all landed in. Every single thing we've been taught about success (and how to get it) has changed. For a long time, we were told there was only ONE main road that led to happiness, accomplishment, and money (and this road was available only to a specific group of privileged people— not women, not people of color, and not people from other marginalized communities). All you had to do was *ease on down this magical yellow brick road* and at the end you'd find a nice house, a new car, a 401(k), health insurance, annual tropical vacations, and maybe even a country club membership all waiting under a rainbow with your name on it. *But hold on a second.* You can't get anywhere near this road unless you go to college first. If you choose a major with great earning potential such as business or finance, or if you plan to go to law school, CONGRATS! You get to pass by all the future waiters and bartenders who majored in liberal arts (like me) and head straight to an internship at a

Fortune 500 company. After you get your diploma, you'll parlay your impressive internships into multiple job offers with decent starting salaries and good benefits. Your parents are going to be soooooooooo proud of you.

You're definitely headed in the right direction because you landed your first "real" job. You and all the other hopeful grads will spend the next few years of your life toiling away in this soul-killing office. Eventually, though, the wheat will be separated from the chaff. *And which one are you?* Do you want to stay in Cubicle-ville forever? Or do you see yourself moving up the proverbial corporate ladder that leads to the office's more expensive real estate? If you want that corner office with a view, DING DING DING, you've made the right choice! Starting right now, you will have to work harder than everyone else. So, when your cowork-ers ask you to join them for two-for-one tequila shots at happy hour, that's a big NO from you. Burning the "midnight fluorescent lighting" eventually pays off with a promotion and a pay increase. Your first big win on the road of life! You repeat the process, buy a house along the way, pay off your student loans, and continue to work the hardest until you get the mother of all promotions. Finally, after years of skipping the tequila and working on week-ends, it's YOUR name on the door of the corner office.

You work even harder in that corner office. You make enough money to buy a lake house, put a couple of kids through college (you knew you were supposed to find a partner and have kids, right?), and replace the Subaru in your driveway with a shiny new Mercedes. Then one day as you gaze at the glorious view from your hard-earned office, you realize, *Oh my God. I have spent thirty-five years toiling away in the promised land that is corporate America! Now what do I do?* Obviously, you saved money like you were supposed to, and thankfully you have a pension because TA-DA, you're ready for the final stage of the journey: RETIRE-MENT. Your colleagues call you into the conference room. There's a big cake and a card. They pop open a bottle of warm champagne and raise their plastic cups to "INSERT YOUR NAME HERE, who never has to work ever again!" YOU DID IT! All that's left to do is pack up your office, drive home in your Mercedes, and order a set of golf clubs from the comfort of your recliner.

THE END.

If you're anything like me, just thinking about a road that leads from graduation and work directly to a water aerobics class in a Florida retirement community makes you want to throw up. Thankfully, NONE of what I just described is true anymore, and there were a few problems with that old road to success anyway. That road was restraining and confining, there wasn't room for everyone, and you were expected to keep your head down as you kept moving forward. If along the way you wanted to try something else, maybe follow your passion for writing or cooking or building interesting furniture, *well then, step aside and enjoy your "artistic" lifestyle, but don't expect to reap the same rewards.* Here's the good news: That old road to success is permanently closed. It has been ripped up and repaved by a new generation of workers who see things differently. Forget the straight lines. The new road has twists and turns, roundabouts, alleyways, and side streets, and *you* get to decide which direction you want to go in. It gets better. That rusty old corporate ladder has been thrown in the trash because we don't need it. We can climb high all on our own. There's more. How many times has someone told you to be patient when it comes to getting ahead in your "career"? Ten, twenty, fifty, more? You don't have to be patient anymore because the tools for getting ahead are readily available and yours for the taking.

And what about "being realistic"? "Be realistic" was practically tattooed on the forehead of every person who took that old-school highway straight to Corporate Land. In Corporate Land you were expected to work hard, have goals, and succeed, *but don't go getting any big ideas.* Keep your head out of the clouds and focus on doing your job even if it bores you to tears. Fast-forward to today and there's no room for basic; thinking big is essential to your survival. And if you are thinking, *Ryan, this doesn't apply to me because I'm really smart and I went to a super impressive Ivy League school where I was tapped for a secret society. So, I'm all set thanks to my big brain, top-notch connections, and six-figure bachelor's degree!* I think it's great that you went to an excellent school and were chosen by an elite group of people to drink beer in a secret dungeon, but what about your skill set? What can you do RIGHT NOW that will make a huge splash? If you're not great at solving problems, making noise, finding creative solutions, thinking miles and miles outside of the box, and just GETTING SHIT DONE, then that ivy-laden degree is about as useful as the VHS tapes in the basement that your mom refuses to throw away.

THE NEW WORLD OF WORK REQUIRES A PERSONAL BRAND

So, hurray! Those old ways of working are over, but what does that actually mean? Whether we like it or not, the new world of work is ultra-fast, competitive, loud, and exciting, and, PS, there has never been a better time for innovators, creators, and rule breakers. It means that curiosity, flexibility, imagination, and the ability to transform ideas into reality are the new version of a top-notch higher education. This is great news, especially for people (like me and you) who would fit into a traditional corporate setting about as easily as an elephant fits into a sports car. However! Succeeding in this new environment, whether you are a 1099 or W-2 employee, means personal brands have never, *ever* been more important. Here's why:

1. No more office hierarchies means rising up *is up to you*. That boring corporate ladder might be gone, but you still need to demonstrate your value if you want to advance professionally.
2. Remote work means that even though you're not chained to a desk all day and there's no micromanager boss hovering over you, you still have to prove to everyone that you're killing it.
3. Social media has connected us all. This means that no matter what line of work you're in, you are now essentially competing with the entire world.
4. It's harder to stand out when standing out has never been more important. We are bombarded with new content constantly, and it takes work to get noticed. People's attention spans are shorter than ever. There are approximately 2.5 quintillion bytes of data created in a single day! Quintillion! Or, as *Medium* helpfully points out, if those bytes were pennies, they'd cover the entire earth five times. Every. Day. Do that many pennies even exist? To cover the entire earth five times EVERY SINGLE DAY?

Again, it doesn't matter what industry you're in, or if you're a 1099 or W-2 worker, there's a huge shift happening, and we all need to be thinking every single day about our personal brands, whether we're selling a service or a product. Nik Sharma points out that a brand "builds affinity between a consumer and the product. In a service business, brand is huge too. Whether you have a service business or a consumer product, developing and building brands builds the loyalty, excitement, and trust which is a huge thing in today's sales environment. Brand is basically the story . . . it's the why." By taking control of our stories and our whys, ultimately we can take control of how we want to be perceived. And do you know what happens if you don't take control of your brand? Someone else will, and who knows what that will lead to? I didn't really want to be "the real estate broker with gray hair," but I became the gray-haired broker because I wasn't 100 percent in control of my brand, since it wasn't my main focus. Please do not allow someone else to brand you "the marketing manager with the overly loud voice" or "the lawyer with the sweaty palms." YOU are the only person who gets to decide which strengths (and weaknesses) you want to embrace and include in the very best version of yourself that you present to the world.

Like many of you, I wasn't interested in following the traditional road to success. If I had tried to, I probably would have ended up on the side of the road begging for a ride so I could get out of there as quickly as possible. Before we move on, here's a quick recap of the early life of Ryan:

1. Was born in Texas and moved eight times before landing in Boston when I was eight.
2. Fell in love with theater in high school.

3. Graduated from college with a degree in theater and English literature.
4. Moved to New York City to become a famous actor.
5. Went to approximately nine million auditions.
6. Played an evil doctor on a soap opera who was murdered by his own grandmother.
7. Played the role of a human clock. My lines were "Tick" and "Tock."
8. Realized I was never ever going to be Tom Cruise.
9. Needed money badly.
10. Bartend or wait tables? *No thank you. Isn't my life already cliché enough?*
11. Spent an hour and a half answering seventy-five multiple choice questions on the New York State real estate exam.

I passed my real estate exam with flying colors and was hired by a brokerage as a new agent. I was no stranger to hard work (remember: nine million auditions!), and I knew I would do whatever it took to be a great agent. I asked lots of questions, read books, shadowed more senior brokers around town, worked long hours, rearranged clients' furniture, fluffed their throw pillows, and swept up the dead cockroaches in their kitchens before showings. I was learning so much and getting better at my job, but there was one enormous obstacle that I didn't know how to get over. That obstacle was ME. I was communicative, positive, reliable, and helpful, but in a city that has over fifty thousand licensed real estate agents, why would anyone choose me? And that's *only* if they were able to find me in the Empire State Building–sized haystack that is full of real estate brokers in New York City. *Why me?* was a hard question to answer. I had little experience, didn't own a suit, wasn't from New York City (I was still learning my way around!), and didn't have a huge network of contacts. So, who cared if I was pretty good at arranging furniture and wasn't afraid of roaches if there was nothing more substantial that made me stand out? What added value could I bring to the table that would make me someone's go-to broker?

There were many steps involved in the transformation of "Ryan Serhant the rookie broker in cowboy boots" to the more refined "Ryan Serhant, CEO of SERHANT. and luxury broker." It didn't happen overnight, but I became the CEO of *the most followed* real estate brand in the world because I was deliberate about building a brand that communicated who I am, what I stand for, and, most importantly, *why I am ALWAYS the go-to person for buying and selling luxury properties.*

When I first started working in real estate, branding was a way of creating my very own playing field when there wasn't much room for me on the team. Back then, I highlighted my relentless work ethic, creativity (especially when it came to making stale listings seem fresh and exciting), negotiation skills, and ability to close deals. Over time, cowboy boots Ryan was gone forever, and my brand continued to evolve and branch out into other areas.

Now SERHANT. is much more than a luxury real estate company. Our mission at SERHANT. is to unite the gig economy using technology through three specific areas: real estate sales, education, and media. We attract buyers, sellers, and customers for our courses and online communities with the content we create in our in-house studio. SERHANT. is part online real estate brokerage, part code academy for sales training, and part HGTV for Gen Z. We are reinventing sales training and defining sales culture for an entirely new generation, and our revenue is generated from real estate brokerage commissions, online course sales, student membership fees, licensing, endorsements, and book sales. That's quite a big switch that's taken place since I was stomping around town in those ridiculous boots.

Now, SERHANT. is the power source that attracts high-end clients who know I am the go-to agent for buying or selling multimillion-dollar properties. It also attracts hungry real estate agents who want to learn more about their craft, sell better, earn more, and be part of a robust community of other salespeople so they can become THE MOST AMAZING versions of themselves. Everything about SERHANT.—our logo, our social media posts, our office space, our partnerships with brands like Chase Bank and Hewlett-Packard, and even the way I dress—is purposeful and supports this idea. As a result, my inbox is always full, my DMs are constant, and the phone does not stop ringing with people who are drawn to our brand and want to hire us or sign up for our courses. The effort we put into the brand pays us back many times over in clients *who come to us.*

The work is worth it, and now it's your turn.

I am going to show you the exact same process I used to dig deep and discover who I am at my core. You're going to learn the same techniques I used to rise above the fray to become *the top* luxury agent and to build a media and real estate company that benefits not only my clients but also other agents. I'm going to walk you through the steps that helped me analyze my goals—what I wanted to achieve, what kind of business I wanted to attract, and what I wanted my future to look like. Together, we are going to crush the *why me?* question by uncovering all your talents, traits, and skills that need to be highlighted. Finally, we are going to take all this information and build a brand that puts you at the top of your game.

The rules are still being written in this new era of working, but one thing is clear: we are not going back to the way things were. Lightning-fast technological advances have revolutionized the workplace. Computers and the internet make connectivity easy—this has improved our productivity, but it also means we are working at a more rapid pace. Globalization allows companies to have access to talent from all corners of the earth, making competition stiffer (and your need to stand out greater). At the time of writing this book, we have also seen enormous companies lay off huge numbers of workers. Meta, Google, Amazon, and many others have laid off thousands and thousands of people.

I had some déjà vu while writing this book too. I started working in real estate on September 15, 2008 . . . the SAME day Lehman Brothers filed for bankruptcy (such a great time to start a new profession!). Now Signature Bank and Silicon Valley Bank have collapsed too. All this volatility serves as a constant reminder that the jobs people are grinding away at might not exist in the near future. Because . . . *who knows?!* It's become almost impossible to depend on one job or one company to employ you forever (but with a solid brand, you don't need to depend on anyone else).

Worker expectations have changed too. All the connectivity enables people to move on from work that isn't fulfilling or doesn't provide growth or opportunities to advance. There's no longer a reason to stick around at a job you don't feel challenged or rewarded by. But make no mistake: it's not that simple. You can't just hurl yourself into the ocean of opportunity and think someone's going to toss you a life raft in the form of your dream job. To survive in this world (whether you're in camp 1099, camp W-2, or both), it is no longer enough to be smart and great at your job. You have to find that extra boost of power if you want to cut through all those big waves and get the success you want. Answering the *why me?* question is the big challenge we all need to face today—no matter what we do. Think about it! Why should someone pick *you* to sell their house, landscape their garden, walk their prize-winning poodle, or invest their money? You might be good at writing, with some published articles under your belt. Maybe you studied the art of landscaping at the palace of Versailles for a decade. Or you're the person who walks all the elite prize-winning pooches. Those are perfectly acceptable reasons for someone to hire you, but without a carefully curated package that shows potential customers who you are, what you do, and *why they should hire you rather than the next person*, you are going to sink to the bottom of this ever-growing sea that is the information economy, where knowledge, information, and services reign supreme.

I'm probably not the first person who has told you that personal branding is important. But I might be the first to say this: good branding is what makes the difference between dreams that are crushed to rubble and dreams that become your reality. I know what it's like to want something different from a prefab, cookie-cutter life. I know how hard it is to accept that your fantasy job isn't going to happen, and you need to find option two. I remember waking up in the middle of the night having NO idea how or where I'd find my next client. It is terrifying to feel like you don't belong and to have no idea what's next. It is frustrating to have great ideas and not know how to get them noticed. It's hard to plan your exit out of a traditional job when you've been there for years and aren't sure where to go. It is scary! But because all of life's big SUPPOSED TOs have been replaced by choices and freedom, we get to control our own narrative, and this changes *everything*. We don't have to be patient or realistic anymore; we don't have to carefully climb a dumb ladder to reach someone else's definition of success. But you need to build your own ladder, and in order to do that you *need to build a brand*.

This journey is all our own. I've never regretted forging my own path, and I'm writing this book for all of you who want to embrace this new landscape and find your own way to shine brighter. Listen to me very carefully. If you don't build a brand that positions you as the go-to makeup artist, graphic designer, accountant, or personal chef, guess what? *It will be someone else.* If you don't use your personal brand as a way to shout about your success from the mountaintop, *no one is going to hear about it* (and that includes your boss and teammates, if you have them). The workplace is like one freshly plucked and absolutely enormous oyster right now, and it's yours for the taking if you put in the work. Don't settle for being second. Don't let yourself get buried by your competition—it's your time to shine. That ember of excitement you feel about your work? It has the potential to start a really big fire, so let's get to it. Let's build your brand and see how high you can go.

CHAPTER 2

Welcome to the SERHANT.
Brand Strategy System

Stop what you're doing. Seriously, just put this book down for a second and look around. What do you see? Whether you're reading or listening to this book in a coffee shop, in the car, on a treadmill, on an airplane, curled up on your sofa at home, or even on a blanket in the middle of a park, you are *surrounded* by brands on all sides. I'm writing this in my office in SoHo right now. This office is full of things that I bought, and everywhere I look, there's a brand: my desk, chair, phone, computer, water bottle, pen, notebook, single-serving bag of Doritos (shhhhhhhh), lucky Tom Brady helmet, and even the music I'm listening to for inspo all represent a choice that was influenced by the way I view certain brands. We all curate our own lives. We can decide exactly how we want our environments to feel, and the choices we make are the result of *how a brand makes us feel*. Doritos make me happy (don't judge—I eat them only on Sundays. I don't want too much red 40 in my diet). And every time I look at Tom Brady's helmet, I think, *Wow, he wasn't picked to play for the Patriots until round six! And now he's got seven Super Bowl rings. Anything is possible, Ryan.* Both Doritos and Tom Brady are brands . . . and

I chose to bring them into my work environment. So, that coffee you're drinking, that airline you picked to fly to Bermuda, that throw pillow under your head, and that banana you're snacking on while sitting in the park? ALL BRANDS. Brands are everywhere, in the form of objects, ideas, services, food, artists, designers, musicians, and athletes. We all like to think we have complete control over our own choices, but we don't (not completely, anyway). Everything we decide to eat, wear, watch, follow, read, and listen to is influenced by branding, and we're going to harness that power to take your business to new heights.

Before we jump into the how-to of brand building together, let's get clear on what a brand actually is and quickly go over the steps we're going to take together to create yours. A quick Google search will pull up more definitions of branding than the total square footage of every co-op in New York City. In other words, *there's a lot of them*. College professors, marketing experts, magazines, newspapers, business journalists, influencers—all of them have their own takes on personal brands. In my interviews with some of the biggest personal brands around, I asked people to share what *brand* means to them:

> **Tom Bilyeu, cofounder of Quest Nutrition and cofounder and host of *Impact Theory*:** "Brand is what other people think about the company you have built. It's both the shout and the echo. The shout is what you do, and the echo is what people think about what you do. *That echo is the brand*."

> **Rebecca Minkoff, designer and founder of the Female Founders Collective:** "When someone closes their eyes, hears a name, and a particular image comes to mind—that's

the brand. In my case, the image we're trying to create in the consumer's mind is downtown, rock 'n' roll, accessible luxury."

Griffin Thall, cofounder and CEO of Pura Vida: "A product that's a brand evokes emotion, it provides an experience, it takes a person out of their day-to-day life. You escape into a feeling from that branded item. When you look down at your wrist and see a Pura Vida bracelet, you're on the beach with your wife or with your family. You're not sitting behind a monitor in an office."

Kenneth Cole, designer and CEO of Kenneth Cole Productions: "A brand is a destination. It has a clear sense of purpose, a reason to exist, and it draws people to it. People aren't inclined to engage with a label, and they want a product for more than what it looks like. It matters how the product makes them feel, how they experience and interact with it."

Gary Vaynerchuk, CEO of VanyerMedia: "Personal brand is an awareness engine."

Lewis Morgan, founder of Gymshark and executive chair of AYBL Group: "Brand is the power that keeps you coming back for more, and it gives you a preemptive vision of what you're getting."

I'm not a college professor, and I didn't go to business school. I haven't spent hours of my life reading journals and writing articles on branding either. But what I have done is plant a tiny seed that I patiently and carefully coaxed into my own billion-dollar brand, and at SERHANT. we define a personal brand as:

> **A carefully cultivated package made up of your strengths, skills, successes, and accomplishments that serves as the foundation of your business. A personal brand allows for an authentic connection with customers, inspires trust and loyalty, and creates greater awareness to attract more business.**

So how do we create that carefully cultivated package through the SERHANT. Brand Strategy System? It starts to take shape as we delve into **Phase One: Discover Your Core Identity**, a.k.a. the special thing that makes you *you*. To discover your core identity, we are going to explore your unique qualities, analyze your greatest skills, and talk about what you are truly, *crazily* passionate about in life. This process is about bringing your most authentic self to the forefront so we can find ways to incorporate those qualities into a great brand that stands out. Eventually, after much soul searching, exploration, and decision-making, a brand is born! You've created something that represents your potential success, and it's almost like holding the Future You right in your own hands. However, keep in mind that your brand is still in its infancy, and it needs a lot of support. You will not experience success if you just throw your brand out into the world all alone like it's Rumspringa.* If you want to grow your brand into

---

* In case you didn't know, Rumspringa refers to a rite of passage among the Amish. Adolescents are given the opportunity to explore the secular world, run wild even, so they can make an informed choice about whether to stay in the Amish community. YES, there are reality shows about this.

a lead-generating machine that brings you an insane amount of positive attention and new business, you need to create a road map that will maximize your brand's power as you usher it into a future where your brand is the GO-TO for whatever it is you do.

Brands are not meant to be flash-in-the-pan, here one day and gone the next. *Remember that one time you saw that cool post on that social media platform? What? You don't?* That's because when there's a GAZILLION bits of data produced every single day you need to be steady and consistent if you want to build a brand that's long-lasting. I think of my personal brand as a living, breathing, ever-changing entity that supports all my business undertakings and creative pursuits. For my brand to keep running smoothly, it needs to be nurtured and fed with consistent content, which is the focus of **Phase Two: Consistency Is the Key**. Without consistent content, your brand will drown in the sea of social media before it even gets a chance to tread water (to be clear, posting content every couple of weeks or when you "feel like it" does not qualify as CONSISTENT). Content creation isn't a 5K you run with a hangover, barely staggering over the finish line while gasping for breath. Consistent content is like running a marathon: it requires steadfast commitment. For the sake of your brand, you have to keep moving NO MATTER WHAT. Before you toss this book aside thinking, *I'm already too busy, Ryan. You lost me at the word "marathon,"* know that we have tactics for streamlining the process so it doesn't take over your entire life. I mean, I want to watch TV too. Don't we all?

Hello, **Phase Three: Shout It from the Mountaintop**! Your brand is out there, and it's gaining traction on social media thanks to all that consistent content you're feeding it. It is gaining more followers, and new leads are practically throwing themselves at your doorstep. Now, listen to me very, very carefully. You have reached a critical junction in the brand-building process, and what you do next determines whether you'll have success . . . or *massive-over-the-top-beyond-your-wildest-dreams SUCCESS*. Which of those two do you want? The latter? Great, now is the time to aim even higher. Here's why. Today, many brands try to live out their entire lives on social media, like it's the final stop on the express train to success. *Wow. We made it this far! This place is fantastic, so let's just stay put.* Sure, it's great to be the king or queen of the internet, but why would you limit yourself? Social media might be the biggest and the easiest party to get into, *but it's not the only party in town*. There are many other ways to gain recognition and amplify your position in your industry. Think of it this way: If a magical genie popped out of your desk drawer and granted you three wishes, would you take ONLY one? *Let's see, hmmmm. Grant me good health, please! I guess I could use the other wishes to create world peace and cure cancer, but I'll just stick with health.* Who would do that when you can have them all? Not pursuing additional opportunities for your brand is like closing the door to more visibility right in the face. This is why the final phase is about being bold and going bigger.

I've been vocal about the fact that I want to be the go-to luxury broker for *the entire world*. That's a lofty goal, and if I want to stand any chance of reaching it, I need to spread my reach as far as I can. Since building my brand, I've branched out and given speeches to huge corporations all over the world, written three books, published articles in online magazines, collaborated with other major brands to produce content, and developed a lucrative education business (and our first class was such a huge hit that the *New York Post* wrote about how much money it brought in on day one, creating even more visibility!). I have also started production on a new TV show, and my business was profiled by *New York Magazine*—the first time they ever profiled a real estate brokerage! If someone had told Ryan-the-rookie-broker that someday he'd be a go-to expert on real estate for the *Wall Street Journal* and CNBC, he would have thought they were delusional. I would have looked down at my khaki pants and my scruffy cowboy boots and thought, *Me? But I share a bathroom in my Koreatown apartment with a dozen other people, and my debit card was just declined at the grocery store while buying tofu and yogurt.*** *I think you've got the wrong guy. Also, can you tell me how to get to Bleecker Street? I'm totally lost! Greenwich Village is so confusing.* This is my way of saying if I can achieve these things, so can you.

If you're thinking, *Yes! I want all those things, but bragging is gross, and it's not cool to talk about your successes like that,* let me enlighten you. If you don't climb up that mountain and shout about your successes to the entire world, no one else is going to do it for you. This phase is about getting loud so you can leverage what you've achieved into press about your company, speaking engagements, writing for publications, collaborations . . . the list goes on and on. Shouting about your accomplishments and branching out and trying new things does not come naturally to many people (and I swear that includes me). But if you don't use your platform to grow bigger and do more, you'll just stay the same. And is that what you want? You're reading this book

---

** True story. I couldn't afford yogurt or tofu. I ran out of the store humiliated and cried about it on the subway.

because you have dreams, and you want success! Growth is not always comfortable!

My business has completely changed since building my personal brand. It has become the glue that holds everything together. My brand is the launching pad that enables me and my team to shoot higher than ever, and it's also the foundation that keeps us focused on our purpose—*being the go-to luxury brokerage for the entire world*. I wanted to write this book because while building a brand can be challenging and overwhelming at times, it isn't one of life's great mysteries (even though it can feel like it). Building a brand is an intentional process—it's the result of careful introspection, hard work, and thoughtful decision-making. The SERHANT. Brand Strategy System lays out a clear path of manageable steps so you can tackle them one by one. All you have to do is follow my lead and be open to huge new possibilities. So, let's do this. Grab your favorite brand of pen, pour yourself your preferred brand of water or coffee, and let's BUILD YOUR BRAND.

PHASE ONE:

Discover Your Core Identity

CHAPTER 3

It's Time to Think Bigger: Creating Your Brand Vision

Here's the thing about the future. Whether or not you've made any plans or given it a single thought, *the future is coming for all of us.* No one gets to have 100 percent control over their own fate. *But.* If you don't take the time to think about what you *really* want from life, then who knows what you'll end up with? Imagine the following scenario: One of your friends decides it would be fun to go see a fortune teller. He drags you into a spooky candlelit storefront, where a mysterious woman in a velvet cloak gestures for you to sit down. She waves her hands around a crystal ball and then gazes into it. She's concentrating intensely . . . like she's about to receive answers to life's most perplexing questions. *Do aliens exist? Is* Million Dollar Listing *really over with season nine or will it be back for more seasons?* After a few seconds she stares deeply into your eyes . . . it's like she's looking directly into your soul. Then she speaks. "I see your future very clearly." You start to get really excited. *She must have seen something amazing! Do I live in a penthouse? Do I drive an expensive car? Am I famous? Wait. Oh my God. Am I the president!?* She takes a dramatic breath and says, "In the future you will walk your dog, go to the grocery store, renew your driver's license, and have regular dental cleanings."

Um, what? Seriously? That's it? Clean teeth and a valid license to drive a motor vehicle? Wow. MY FUTURE SUCKS. You'd want a refund, right? That's because deep down we all expect that our futures will be bright and exciting. Think about it. No one fills a vision board with pictures of people folding laundry. If you were at a job interview and someone asked, "Where do you see yourself in five years?" you wouldn't say, *I see myself watching television all day long.* That's because whether we are aware of it or not, we are all capable of big things, and we expect more from our lives than basic trips to the grocery store. But for whatever reason, we don't always take the necessary steps to create a mind-blowing, envy-inducing future for ourselves. In our ultra-fast-insta-famous society, it's so easy to think that there's a ceiling on success—that our greatest desires are out of reach. But it's not true! There is no limit to what you can achieve if you take the time to deliberately build a brand. You can start getting that brand recognition you want RIGHT NOW. It starts by having high expectations for yourself and making a commitment to do some soul searching about what matters to you The Most.

I suck at sports—I was always the last kid standing when it came to picking teams in gym class. While I hope to never touch a baseball glove ever again, I do believe there is much wisdom to be gleaned from sports. Yogi Berra famously said, "If you don't know where you are going, you'll end up someplace else." True enough (and thank God for GPS). I'd like to take this idea a little further. If you don't know what you *truly* want and what you stand for, you'll end up spending your entire life doing . . . WHO THE HELL KNOWS? Again, that brand is already inside of you, waiting for you to take control. It's not going to arrive at your front door like a FedEx package. Brands require a real thought process, and you have to take control! Steve Jobs didn't wake up one morning and think, *Oh, it's Thursday. My calendar is wide open, so what should I do today? I guess I'll get rid of all my shoes and then I'll create a technology brand that will change the way the entire world thinks, works, communicates, and entertains themselves!* Ole Kirk Kristiansen, the Danish builder who invented Legos, didn't throw down his hammer in disgust and think, *Screw carpentry. I'm so over it. I know what might be fun! I'll make a toy that is excruciatingly painful for people to step on while walking to the bathroom in the middle of the night. I'll make a fortune!* Those legendary brands were sparked by a vast viewpoint of a bright future and strong values.

If you want to be a go-to brand in your field, you need to know what you want and what you stand for and be willing to take your ideas to a higher level so you can act on them. These concepts serve as the basis for a brand vision statement. **A brand vision statement is a written description of your brand's purpose, intentions, and goals for the future.** Think of a brand vision statement like a reduction a chef makes on your favorite cooking show. You mix your key ingredients together (viewpoint and values) and let them all simmer until they've been boiled down to an intensely flavored concentrate. The gold you get from that reduction? That's the *flavor* of your future brand—it's the special essence that will allow you to create a strong brand vision statement that will serve as your ticket to success. Relax, you don't literally have to cook anything, but if you don't know what your viewpoint and values are you're basically throwing a bunch of random things in a pot and hoping for the best. So, what do you want? You can be a sloppy, half-assed mystery stew . . . or you can be a carefully crafted sauce that *everyone wants to taste.* I mean, do you even need to think about this? Let's get cooking. It's time to find your three special ingredients and make some magic.

Formula "V": The Essence of a Go-To Brand

The formula here is:
VIEWPOINT + VALUES = BRAND VISION STATEMENT

VIEWPOINT

On a basic level, a viewpoint acts as a source of inspiration. If you've ever watched the sun go down over the Grand Canyon, or maybe stood on the observation deck of the Eiffel Tower with all of Paris spread out before you, you know that a great view can be awe-inspiring. I see plenty of views in my line of work, but the first time I saw the view from my $250 million listing in Central Park Tower, which sits 1,416 feet above Billionaires' Row, I was too blown away to speak (I have never been rendered mute by a view before; it's that crazy). This eight-bedroom, seven-bathroom, ultra-*ultra*-luxurious home is 17,545 square feet spread out over three floors and is the highest residence in the entire country. It also has the highest outdoor terrace IN THE ENTIRE WORLD.

One of my mantras in my early days of selling real estate was "Expansion always, in all ways," and the view from Central Park Tower is like my mantra coming to life. When I'm standing on the highest terrace in the world, it feels like I can see forever; unlimited possibility surrounds me on all sides. I worked long and hard on my brand to get the most expensive listing in the country, and that mind-blowing view has become a powerful reminder that there is nothing I can't accomplish. There is nothing that is too big or too out of reach for SERHANT.

To create a go-to brand that brings you the big income, you've got to let your mind open up and expand to everything that's possible *long before you're able to make it a reality*. Think about it: Have you ever bought clothes for a friend's newborn baby? I don't think anyone walks into a store that sells baby clothes and says, "My friend's new baby weighs seven pounds and six ounces and is nineteen and a half inches long. I need clothes for those exact measurements." We don't do this because we all know that baby is going to grow (and fast), so we buy clothes that will fit a twenty-pound baby, which is more than double its current size. If your personal brand is in its infancy, assume it will be huge in due time if you put in the work. And you need a viewpoint that inspires you, guides you, and serves as a constant reminder of what is possible in order for your brand to reach its maximum potential. In other words, GO BIGGER. My view from that jewel of an apartment way up in the sky is a HUGE motivator. I can close my eyes, *like right now*, and picture how tiny Manhattan looks from that unbelievable height that my brand has taken me to, and I am instantly reminded of my goals.

Building a brand is hard work, and your viewpoint can also provide a much-needed push to keep going when you need it. I love my work, but like everyone else, I still have those *what was I thinking?* moments after a tough day. A difficult client, a lost deal, the never-ending to-do list that comes along with being a CEO. Sometimes it's easy to think, *Well, today sucked. Seriously, I've had it. I'm going to pack my bags and move my family to a small island in Greece, grow back the beard, and spend the rest of my life wearing shorts, riding around on a scooter, and trying to learn Greek.* But before I burn all my suits and ties on a pyre, I take a breath, picture that unbelievable view, and let the stress and anxiety roll off my tightly wound shoulders. My viewpoint helps me picture success—SERHANT. dominates the industry. There are SERHANT. signs in front yards across the entire country. Our logo with the signature SERHANT. blue is as recognizable as the Nike swoosh. Our education division is teaching people all over the world the essential skills they need to be great at sales, build a brand, and run a business. We're still producing high-quality content for our social channels, and we're using it to sell more properties than anyone else. Soon enough I'm back on track and no longer thinking about running off to an island in Greece. (Note to self, cancel plane tickets. Don't buy any more shorts.) The excitement about the future of SERHANT. is so much bigger than the stress of a client who wants to back out of their contract because the lobby in the condo building of the $20 million apartment they're buying has questionable feng shui. I dust myself off and get back in the game.

Your viewpoint doesn't have to come from an actual view or an image in your head of you driving around in your dream car. Your incentivizing viewpoint can be a mission. Maybe you can imagine what the world would be like if you solved a big problem that you care about deeply. Imagining how you can improve life for yourself, your loved ones, and all of humanity can be the positive viewpoint that keeps you moving forward.

Tom Bilyeu, cofounder of Quest Nutrition and cofounder and host of *Impact Theory*, has a deep purpose he describes as "helping people optimize their life for fulfillment. Everything we do at Quest is about this; it is my anchor. I wanted to build something that really matters and fight for something I believe in. I grew up in a morbidly obese family, and I wanted to help my family by making food they could choose based on taste that happened to be good for them." Bilyeu credits imagining how his product would help his family as a huge driver that got him through the roughest times of building his brand. "You have to believe in something that you're willing to really fight for. My belief made me feel like a warrior. I could go into the fight feeling like I'm not just doing this for me, I'm going this to help the people I am here to serve." Bilyeu believes all entrepreneurs face a moment when they are about to give up, and you need to have that viewpoint to save you. "There has to be a pretty profound reason why you're going to keep doing what you're doing, and money isn't going to be enough. I know people think it will, but it won't help you past a certain point, and you're going to ask the question, 'Why am I doing this?' It was my vision that got me past that question when it was two o'clock a.m. on a Friday and I was in a warehouse with bloody knuckles from a wrapping machine." Your vision for your brand needs to be big and colorful enough to carry you past obstacles . . . including bleeding all over yourself in the middle of the night while your friends are out partying (or at home sleeping).

NOW IT'S YOUR TURN

Exercise: YOU Are the Headline

This exercise is going to help you THINK BIGGER so you can come up with a viewpoint that will serve as the launching pad for your brand vision statement.

Remember the THREE essential qualities of an effective brand vision statement:

Future focused: Focus on what you want your brand to look like five years from now. Really see it. It should look great!

Aspirational, but doable: You want to really push yourself, but you want to stay in the realm of possibility based on where you are today. For example, creating an invisibility cloak might not be a reasonable goal for you right now.

Simple, clear, and logical: This shouldn't be overly complex; it should make sense to you, your clients, your mom, your roommates, and random people on the street.

Imagine Yourself in the Not-So-Distant Future

Now, imagine yourself five years into the future. After another incredible year of massive success, you've made the cover of the most respected newspaper or magazine in your local market. Think about how amazing you look on that cover and how great it feels to see your hard work bringing in so much media attention. As you're reveling in your future success, contemplate the following questions:

1. What does the headline of the article say?

2. What are the keywords that describe your brand in the article?

3. According to this fictional but glowing article, who are your clients? What is it about your brand that makes you so successful?

4. What is the value your brand has brought to your customers and clients?

5. Keeping your answers to all these questions in mind, describe what your business will look like five years down the road.

Values Are at the Heart of Your Brand

Your core values are the pulse that runs through everything you do as you work hard to bring your vision for your brand to light. Your values are an expression of your purpose, and they will keep you grounded even though you are reaching for something that can feel insanely high up. Your values trickle down and impact every aspect of your brand. They determine your brand's priorities and influence how team members interact with each other (if you have them). Your values provide parameters for how you form relationships with clients whether you are a dog walker, a graphic designer, or a restaurateur with a full staff. In other words, *your values dictate how clients experience your brand.*

Mike Evans, cofounder of GrubHub and founder of Fixer, realized early on that taking full responsibility for the customer experience was the value that would be a crucial part of their success: "If people got food and it was either low quality, the delivery was slow, or there was a mistake, people said, 'GrubHub screwed up.' Initially

I thought, 'We're not cooking the food. We're delivering it.' But instead of trying to fight the consumer assumption that Grub-Hub gets both the credit and the blame, we built the entire company around our food. The food coming from GrubHub is going to be better, faster, hotter, and higher quality than if you get it from a place other than GrubHub. Delivering the best food became one of GrubHub's core values, and it defined the brand. Owning that customer, acknowledging that they're a GrubHub customer and not a restaurant customer, means we will never let them go. I will never let another customer service department talk to them. We took responsibility for the food order, and we were never going to outsource the experience. That was the brand."

Clarifying your values also helps determine the attitude and the energy you want your brand to exude. When a group of people are united behind a purpose—whether it's to sell real estate or create the universe's greatest chocolate chip cookie—the positivity becomes infectious, fueling your mission. When we wrote our values at SERHANT., I knew I wanted them to promote **togetherness**, **mutual support**, and **hard work**. A feeling of positivity and being focused on what we can achieve together *in the future* was also important to me.

SERHANT. Values

Amplify together: We support each other at our low points, and we never let our high points go to our heads. If one of us is behind, we are all behind. And when one of us succeeds, we ALL do.

Create for tomorrow: We are future obsessed and always look forward, creating to bring the future to today.

Be relentless: We are not only tireless in the pursuit of achieving our goals, we are tenacious seekers of knowledge, never sacrificing personal growth for professional growth.

Disrupt for good: We are the best at what we do because we never lose sight of the people and communities around us. Our voice carries above the rest, and we disrupt to have a positive, lasting impact.

As you begin this process, never forget that customers *pay for values*. Values matter more to consumers now than they ever have before. Brands like Warby Parker and Tom's Shoes became known for their "buy one give one" approach. If someone said, "Hey, love your new glasses!" or "Cute shoes!" that compliment came with the added bonus of knowing your purchase got glasses or shoes to someone in need. Consumers care about values such as carbon footprints, ethical sourcing, and social impact. Values are so important that billions of dollars can be lost and a brand can be permanently damaged due to what some consumers view as a lapse in values (as we've recently seen with major beer and shoe brands).

Think about what kind of experience you want to create for your clients and customers. While the end goal of all this work is to build a successful brand that will increase business, establishing your brand's values is about putting your feet into the customer's shoes before they buy your product or service. What is it like being in those shoes? How does it feel? Neil Brown, CEO of Amsale, says *how the bride felt* throughout her experience with the brand was their main focus. "Amsale always articulated that her inspiration was the bride, and she was extraordinarily empathetic with clients. She would try to envision what the customer was feeling and thinking as she was trying on dresses. 'Does this dress make her feel confident? Does she feel beautiful?' Amsale wanted to make dresses that framed the bride as the center of attention, and she wanted the bride to feel comfortable in that role." Neil explains that this value of empathy is woven throughout the customer's entire experience at Amsale. "When a bride comes into our store, we want her to feel like she's meeting someone who understands her and can help her fulfill her vision. This starts the moment she arrives, when our team members greet her and then listen to her thoughts and ideas so they can choose dresses that will bring her vision to life." Articulating your brand's values is about articulating the experience you want all your clients and customers to have.

NOW IT'S YOUR TURN

Exercise: Visualize Every Moment

Now we're going to dig deeper. Close your eyes and imagine you are a customer seeking out the exact service or product you offer. Picture the client or customer as they experience every aspect of your brand—logging on to your website, taking a meeting with you in a coffee shop, or walking into your physical office for the first time. Contemplate the following and write down the ideal experience you want your customers to have:

What do they see? A well-designed website that is attractive, informative, and easy to navigate? A bridal shop that is light and airy? A café that's buzzing with activity, people working on laptops or having animated conversations, plates of delicious-looking food everywhere? A smiling face that greets them at the local Starbucks where you're meeting to discuss dog-walking services?

What do they feel? Pulling the right emotions out of your clients is an essential part of your brand experience. Is a bride's anxiety about planning her wedding being soothed? Does the café environment make a customer feel welcome and at home? Does the pleasant conversation and the positivity of the dog walker make the proud Labradoodle owner think, *Oh, Muffin will be in great hands with this dog walker*?

How will you make the full experience a reality?
Now that you've imagined what it's like for a customer to walk into your office, engage your services, or log on to your website, ask yourself what key values need to be in place in order to make that experience a reality. For example, I knew if I wanted to be the go-to brand for luxury properties, I'd always have to be looking forward . . . using media in the most innovative way to sell properties, always up on different ways to reach a global audience to get our listings in front of the most eyes. I knew that SERHANT. needed to be "future focused," so "create for tomorrow" is one of our core values. Our clients know that SERHANT. will always use the most innovative, creative, and groundbreaking methods to get properties sold for millions and millions of dollars.

PRO TIP: VALUES ARE IMPORTANT IF YOU'RE GOING TO BUILD A HEALTHY TEAM

If you already have a team, it's also important to think about how your values and your team can work together to make your brand a success. How can your values be used to set priorities? Think about the work ethic you want to model. How can you use your values to keep everyone motivated? And most importantly, ask yourself if you would want to work for your own brand. Analyze the qualities that make YOU want to be part of your own business. . . . Is it the value of service or dedication? Knowing what values will draw talent to your company will help you focus on maintaining an environment that supports your team members so they can do their best work.

You've established your viewpoint and contemplated the values your brand needs to accomplish your goals. Now it's time to take those concepts and craft a written description of your brand's purpose, intentions, and goals for the future. Before you write up a brand vision statement and get it tattooed across your chest, there's a few things you need to know:

The Elements of a Brand Vision Statement

When creating a brand vision statement, use the following parameters:

1. **Future focused:** Your vision statement is a proclamation of what your brand will achieve in the next three to five years.

2. **Sets the bar at the right height:** This is an aspirational statement. You're declaring what it is you're reaching for, and it's big, but it's not over-the-top crazy. It must *actually be possible* to achieve your vision within the correct time frame (it took longer than three years to split the atom). A brand vision statement is where possibility meets reality.

3. **Uses your heart, not your head:** Practicality serves no purpose here. What your partner, friends, or family *think you should want* doesn't matter. What you *think you should want* isn't what we're talking about either. This is not the time to hold back. Your brand vision statement needs to authentically represent you. This is about something you want so badly you can practically taste it, hear it, touch it, and see it.

4. **It's all for you:** There's a reason I told you not to get a tattoo. This isn't something you need to share with the world. This is a tool to keep you focused and on track as you build your brand. Your brand vision statement will likely evolve over time—and that's fine! This is for you, and you can change it along the way.

5. **Is worth fighting for:** The vision you create should inspire and excite you EVERY SINGLE DAY. It also aligns with your values. Your brand means everything. It's like fine art, a vintage car, a rare bottle of wine, a flawless diamond. . . . *It is precious to you.*

Before you completely freak out and claim to have writer's block, know that this statement is only a couple of sentences long. You don't have to fret about writing a gloriously articulate statement either—there are no literary awards for best brand vision statement. Clear and simple is your mantra. Your main objective is to combine your VIEWPOINT and your VALUES to create your statement. Then you can plan the necessary steps to make them a reality, hold yourself accountable, and monitor your own progress. Let me show you what I mean. I came up with the following brand vision statement for SERHANT.:

> **Be globally recognized for selling the world's most expensive properties with the world's wealthiest clients in the next three to five years.**

Let's break that down.

It's future focused: I know where I'd like to be, and three to five years is a reasonable time frame based on where I am today. I'm not brand-new to the game, so this leap is doable in theory.

It's a very, very high bar—but it's not impossibly high. Jeff Bezos hasn't picked up the phone and asked me to find him a new house. However, I have a solid track record of selling luxury properties to high-net-worth individuals, including one of the most expensive houses in the entire country.

This is what my heart wants, there's no question about it. Nothing scares me more than unrealized potential, and if I'm going to spend my entire life (and there are years and years of my life left!) selling real estate, then why settle for being good? I want to be the best. I want to sell the most spectacular properties in the world to the people who can afford to buy them.

That statement is for me. I have it memorized. I can write it forward and backward. Again, it's not permanent and it can

evolve, but for now that statement perfectly sums up everything I want to achieve over the next few years. I refer to it ALL
THE TIME.

Last, when I read my brand vision statement, I actually get
chills. Just the words *globally recognized* make me think, *Hell
yes! This is exactly what I want to be known for!* And isn't that
the point of all this? Doing the work to create this statement puts
you in a position to build the business that you want to build, so
get to it!

BRAND VISION STATEMENTS FROM SOME OF OUR FAVORITE BRANDS

Mike Evans, cofounder, GrubHub, and founder, Fixer
"High-quality food at home, as good as you can get in a restaurant."

Justina Blakeney, founder, Jungalow
"Jungalow is freedom. Jungalow is the wild, innate, nature-filled life that's inside of you. It's the warmth, coziness, and safety of home. It's bringing out who you are in your own environment."

Griffin Thall, cofounder and CEO, Pura Vida
"Make people feel like they're on vacation with their best friends, living free, and living life to the fullest."

NOW IT'S YOUR TURN

Exercise: Creating Your Brand Vision Statement

Listen, while this exercise is meant to be simple, that doesn't mean it is easy. Take your time and don't stress it. Sit with it, draft it, tweak it, revisit it. When we worked on our brand vision statement at SERHANT., we spent HOURS talking, examining, imagining, pondering, crossing out ideas, rewriting ideas, taking snack breaks, and talking some more. While this statement is FOR YOU, it is also a touchstone that has the power to help you guide your brand to greatness. I recommend having a protein shake while you work on this—it takes energy! Also, follow the steps below:

1. **Transform that viewpoint into a mission.**
    Think of phrases like *make people feel, inspire, be recognized as, be the go-to, provide comfort, solve, help with, transform, disrupt, change,* etc.
2. **Establish who your focus is.** Think, *gifted children, families, couples, struggling students, teachers, concerned parents, the wealthy, passionate cooks, animal lovers, the food insecure, people who want to be healthier, busy moms,* etc.
3. **Identify the what.** This is where you articulate what your brand will do. Think, *provide study skills,*

> *offer vegan catering, plan travel experiences, design*
> *gardens, sell properties, provide childcare, etc.*
>
> 4. **Add a modifier.** Now you need to add a modifier
> to indicate how what your brand does is special.
> Think, *efficient, increase, farm to table, adventurous,*
> *sustainable, flexible, expensive, accessible, custom-*
> *made, bespoke, tailored,* etc.
>
> 5. **Top it off with a time frame.** The key here is to
> give yourself a reasonable time frame. You want to
> push yourself but also exist in the realm of possibility.
>
> 6. **Put it all together in a statement that's**
> **meaningful to you.**
> *"Be the Chicago area's most sought-out caterer for*
> *vegan farm-to-table catering by the end of the year."*
> *"Be the country's go-to affordable, dependable*
> *delivery service in the next three to five years. "*
> *"Be recognized as the leading expert in effective*
> *study skills for gifted children within five years."*

Amazing things really can happen when you open up your mindset and push yourself to dream big, and I would never have made it onto the world's highest terrace if I hadn't been so committed to the idea of my brand's growth. In September 2020, the *Wall Street Journal* did an article on my brand-new baby brokerage. Life was insane in the fall of 2020. New York City was shut down, and countless storefronts were boarded up. There was a curfew to keep people off the streets, and the sound of emergency vehicle sirens replaced the noise of honking traffic.

That was what life was like in New York City when that article came out. One of the things the article discussed was SERHANT. Signature, our private client division for buyers and sellers in the $10 million+ bracket. This division provides premium white-glove services and a team of experts that specialize solely in high-end listings. Clients in our Signature division get customized websites, expert video tours, and access to me at the drop of a hat. Signature also offers concierge services to these clients. Need help fixing the media system in your private jet? We'll figure that out. Reservations at impossible-to-get-into restaurants? We WILL find a way. I knew it was important to have a separate upscale marketing strategy for this arm of my brand, but I had zero idea that Signature (and that *Wall Street Journal* article) would result in the giant stamp of approval my brand-new business needed.

A few days after the article came out, I got a call from a concierge service in Manhattan (these are services that help the extra rich with *anything*). They wanted to know if I could find a rental for one of their high-net-worth clients. My answer was YES, even though I thought my rental days were behind me. But between the responsibility of the new business, the crazy environment of the city, and my now enormous payroll, I wasn't about to say no. My new client, who I'll call Mr. Q, had a rental budget of about $50,000 (that is per month, by the way). To get to the good part of this story (where my mind is utterly blown), I'm going to quickly summarize the events:

1. We find Mr. Q a rental, but it is so expensive, and buying would be cheaper. Plus, EVERYTHING IN THE CITY IS CLOSED. I have to ask, "Do you really need

to be here right now? Have you thought about Florida? Florida has great options. You can live anywhere! I could send over some property info for you to look at."

2. Mr. Q is open to Florida. I'm surprised that he looks at the properties I send right away. He calls and says, "Meet me in Florida on Thursday. Palm Beach! Not Miami. Miami isn't for me."

3. I've done deals in Florida before, but I don't know it the way I know New York City. I go bonkers learning every single detail I can about Florida. I know everything. Questions about airspace (this is a concern if you are near Mar-a-Lago), schools, and the best places to eat. If Mr. Q wants a gluten-free croissant and a cup of coffee made from beans grown by fairies on a mountainside in Peru, I've got it under control.

4. I fly to Florida fully masked, but I do not wear the hazmat suit like Emilia suggests.

5. I've scheduled several showings of great properties, but SHIT. One of them has to change the time, and there is now an awkward gap in our schedule, and I don't know what to do. . . . *Wait! I'll do a Wow Moment*. I'll take him to see that ultra-luxurious house that's on the market for a massive NINE FIGURES.

ENTER THE WOW MOMENT

The Wow Moment is a sales technique I use frequently (I talk about it in *Sell It Like Serhant*). It involves blowing someone's mind at the beginning of a property search by showing them an option that is out of their price range. *Why would you do that, Ryan?* I do it because the Wow Moment is a means of showing a client that if they want Property A, they need to be open to spending more money because the options in their price range do not allow for this level of luxury. This can result in (1) *Oh, so if I spent X amount more, I could have all this?* And their wallet falls open. OR (2) *I definitely can't afford this, but now that I've seen what is available in my range, I'll stretch just a tiny bit more.* The Wow Moment is also a time-saver, because seeing how much luxury *really costs* immediately prevents some buyers from walking into a lower-priced apartment and saying, "No way! Where's the rooftop deck, pool, gym, billiard room, and dog playground?" The Wow Moment sets a buyer's expectations on the right track by showing how far a budget can actually go. The Wow Moment is a very useful sales tool, and it's the exact same technique that resulted in my dropping $200 more than I was planning to on a pair of shoes when I first started selling real estate (the salesperson who showed me those Prada loafers—a.k.a. the Wow Shoe— was a sales GENIUS). There was no way I could afford the Prada shoes, but I did realize it was worth stretching my budget to get something of a higher quality than my original choice. Try it!

I take Mr. Q to see a house that is THE DEFINITION OF WOW.* Before we go in, I say, "You're not going to buy this one. It's three times more than what you want to pay, but it's incredible and I want you to see it." Honestly, I've seen some crazy houses, but I have never seen anything like this. Everything about this house makes other houses look . . . just sad. Walking into the wow house is like passing out in dusty old Kansas and waking

---

* The WOW house had an asking price of $140 million. Insane right?!

up in Technicolor Oz. The house is *otherworldly*. I am like a kid who is so overly excited that they can't get their words out fast enough. . . . *WOW. This room is insane. Do you see that view of the ocean? The sand is so white it looks like an ultra-soft carpet. Wait. Is that? AN AQUARIUM?* The wow house is so serene, and the aquarium so beautiful . . . I swear the fish inside of it swim better than other fish. I stand there wide-eyed, not moving, because honest to God if I was ever going to see a mermaid it was going to be RIGHT THERE IN THAT AQUARIUM. The parade of marvels continues. The gym makes Equinox look like your uncle's dirty garage where he keeps a rusty old weight bench. The closet makes Bergdorf Goodman look like a Salvation Army. The light is better; the air is fresher! I never, ever want to leave this house, and I can tell Mr. Q loves it too. But we have to move on. Sadly, all Wow Moments have to come to an end.

I take Mr. Q to look at the other properties. The first one is $53 million. He takes one step into the house, does an about-face, and gets right back in the car. *Um, so you didn't like this one?* It gets worse. When we get to the next house, which is $35 million, HE WON'T EVEN GET OUT OF THE CAR. I am starting to panic. Have I been betrayed by the Wow Moment? Did I fly all the way down here in the middle of a plague just to screw things up with this client? I get back in the car, and he says, "Get me the other one." I'm puzzled. *The one you exited so fast, it was like you'd stumbled into a hoarder's lair that was overrun with cats?* "The first one. Get me the first one. What's it worth?"

My mind is spinning. . . . "Great. I'll get you comps." *Do we have comps for a place that is the Garden of Eden, Shangri-La, and the Palace of Versailles all wrapped up in one?* A negotiation follows, a contract is signed, a wire is sent . . . and just a few days after SERHANT. Signature got a call about a rental, I have sold the most expensive residential property in the entire country.** I can't believe what is happening. I call Emilia, and I send emails to my team to share the news about SERHANT.'s first big sale. Once I return to earth, I take myself to the restaurant at the hotel and order steak and lobster to celebrate. I have just sold one of the most expensive residential properties in the world (in the depths of COVID), and this record-breaking deal is an enormous validator for my new company. I feel like I have a huge stamp on my forehead that says SERHANT. IS THE GREATEST COM-PANY OF ALL TIME. After my decadent dinner, I walk along the beach, looking out at the ocean. The sun is just starting to set. As the sun dips into the Atlantic, I think, *Wow, that was spectacular!* I turn around and walk back to my hotel. . . . I can't wait to see what SERHANT. can do next.

You have no idea how far your brand can take you. I'm com-fortable having big dreams and pushing myself, but it's the foun-dation of my brand that has enabled me to climb higher than I ever could before. The power to dream big exists inside all of us, but you need to believe that whatever it is you imagine—being the CEO of your own company, a best-selling writer, a principal of a school, a tech entrepreneur, a filmmaker, the chef at your own restaurant—ANYTHING IS AVAILABLE TO YOU. This is the first big step on your journey to building an unstoppable brand, so go big, be bold, and know you have the ability to climb as high as you want to.

** After negotiations it sold for $122.7 million.

Congratulations on getting your brand-building process off the ground. Look what you've accomplished so far:

Used Formula "V": The Essence of a Go-To Brand to:
      Establish your viewpoint ✔
      Identify your values ✔
      Craft your brand vision statement ✔

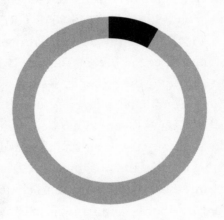

NOW IT'S SYDNEY'S TURN

EXERCISE: YOU ARE THE HEADLINE

Headline: The Nation's Top Trainer Helps Clients Build Their Best SELF

Keywords: Game-changing, confident, empowering, strong

Clients, Type of Business, Success: Sydney Sherman of Self by Syd coaches clients around the world to step into their power by taking control of their health and wellness routines.

How do you describe your business at that moment? Self by Syd started as a ten-week program to empower clients with awareness of their own wellness routines and how those routines can affect mental and physical well-being. Since its inception, Self by Syd has grown into an international brand, helping millions cut out the noise and craft a lifestyle that makes them feel strong, amplifies their success, and raises their confidence to soaring heights.

Formula "V": Viewpoint + Values

I've been athletic my entire life, but after I aged out of competitive dance, I remember how confusing it felt to understand what exercises, meals, and habits were best for me. I followed countless influencers with "perfect" bodies, spent SO MUCH money on online programs, and read stacks of conflicting papers to even just *try* to understand nutrition.

After a grueling, yearslong journey through every wellness fad imaginable, I finally said to myself, "If none of this is making ME feel good, why am I doing it?" And from that point on, I shifted my focus entirely to myself—I brought awareness to what types of movement energized me, what types of food made me feel nourished and not bloated and did not leave me hungry, what schedules kept me feeling rested and productive . . . and thus, Self by Syd was born!

My mission is to provide trustworthy, accessible education and programming to help people like me—who are ready to commit to themselves but don't know where to start—understand how to approach wellness in a way that's unique and highly personalized.

That's what gets me up and to the gym at 5:00 a.m. on freezing New York City mornings. :)

Brand Vision Statement Exercise

1. **Transform that viewpoint into a mission.**
   a. Disrupt the industry by helping people feel like they have the tools to take control of their health and wellness.
   b. Give people the confidence to craft a wellness routine that makes them feel their best.
   c. Empower people to look internally before using outside resources, like influencers, when deciding how to approach their own health and wellness.
2. **Establish who your focus is.**
   Busy people who want to live happier, healthier, more productive lives.

3. **Identify the what: This is where you articulate what your brand will do.**
   Give busy people the education and guidance they need to feel confident in the decisions they make to live happier, healthier, more productive lives.

4. **Add a modifier: Now you need to add a modifier to indicate how what your brand does is special.**
   a. Accessible
   b. Customizable
   c. Empowering

5. **Top it off with a time frame: The key here is to give yourself a reasonable time frame. You want to push yourself but also exist in the realm of possibility.**
   I'd love to create a market for personalized wellness and influence the "influencer" industry for health and fitness by 2030.

6. **Put it all together in a statement that's meaningful to you.**
   Be recognized as the go-to brand for trustworthy, accessible education and programming to help craft a unique, highly personalized approach to wellness by 2026.

Sydney's Brand Vision Statement

Empowering the world to build their best Self.

CHAPTER 4

The *AND* Behind Your Brand: Finding Your Superpower

When two different things are paired together, the ordinary can be transformed into something truly special. Nothing says "happy Saturday morning" like a big fluffy stack of Pinterest-worthy pancakes. But before I dig in, *would someone please pass the syrup*? Everyone knows that it's pancakes *and* maple syrup that are the real winning combo. The same is true of so many things: movies and popcorn, hot chocolate and marshmallows, tequila and lime, and can we all agree that Tuesdays are better with tacos? Great pairings are by no means limited to food; the right match can make people stronger and more interesting too. Thelma was a bored, miserable housewife until she went on a road trip with a friend . . . then things got pretty spicy for Thelma *and* Louise. Sherlock Holmes might have been a genius, but most people found him unbearably obnoxious until he partnered up with a more genial doctor. Together, Sherlock Holmes *and* Dr. Watson became an unstoppable crime-solving duo. Then there's Drake Parker. *Wait a second, who?* See? Drake barely exists without "*and* Josh."

The AND in all these statements is so much more than a conjunction. **The word AND is connecting two entities that complement each other, maximizing their best qualities to form a unique and ultra-powerful combination.** Stick with me on this. Take the classic peanut butter and jelly. What happens if you remove the jelly from the equation? You're left with a dry, boring sandwich that will immediately glom onto the roof of your mouth. *No thank you, and where's my water bottle?* Sometimes AND is the key to bringing out something's true sparkle and shine. I'm going to lead you to your AND, so you can take this extra dose of magic and make your personal brand bigger and more impactful.

While I was building SERHANT. I was especially conscious of one thing: I needed to stand out in a *very* large crowd. I'm talking a football-stadium-size crowd. There are approximately 80,000 real estate agents in New York City. To give you a sense of how bananas that is, even in a city with a whopping population of over 8 million, there is one real estate agent for every 105 people! THE RATIO OF REAL ESTATE BROKERS TO HUMANS IN THIS CITY IS INSANE. If I wanted to take every single agent in this city to a Buccaneers game in Tampa, *I couldn't because Raymond James Stadium fits only 65,326 people.* And every single one of these agents is trying to sell properties in the same measly 22.82 square miles that make up Manhattan. I knew that if I wanted to get closer to making my brand vision a reality, I had to find a way to cut through all this noise. The question was, how could I do that in a way that would stick? I already had a visible presence in the industry. I had been on TV for years and written books and articles, had a large social media following and billions of dollars in sales under my belt, and our house tours were becoming increasingly popular on TikTok. I also had a reputation for being a guy who isn't afraid to add just a little dash of crazy to his sales and marketing tactics. You want me to sell your apartment across the street from Manhattan's famed Lincoln Center? On it. . . . But first, pass me that tutu! Your apartment has zero light? No problem—I'll find a vampire willing to pay cash. Oh! You live on Great Jones Street? Step aside as I draw potential buyers to your historic property by embodying Samuel Jones, New York State assemblyman from 1796 to 1799, first city comptroller, and "father of the New York bar." Jeez, the things you have to do in this town to get a street named after you. I like to get edgy with social media posts too. In our "happy Thanksgiving" post I climbed onto the roof of our headquarters in SoHo and roasted a turkey with a flamethrower (note to self: answer accountant's email to say that yes, it was me who put the flamethrower on the corporate Amex). I've always been imaginative, and I love tapping into my creative side to make sales, but I'd be kidding myself if I thought wearing ridiculous costumes was going to help me get closer to my brand vision. That worked as a way to break out of the crowd when I was getting started, but at a certain point I needed to go bigger with my vision and needed a new angle if I wanted to emerge as *the* luxury broker in a crowd that's bigger than the entire city of Scranton, Pennsylvania.

What could I do differently? This question was like my own personal plague, infecting my every thought. I pondered this problem while I was at the gym, in the shower, brushing my teeth, stuck in traffic, and just walking around the streets of New York City. I had NO ideas. I was starting to worry I'd have to do something desperate like start riding around town on a horse— but that's just being wacky, isn't it? I wanted to be authentic but also an elevated version of my admittedly quirky self. . . . *But who was that guy in the tutu, and why do people want to buy luxury properties from him?* One afternoon, as I got out of the car in front of my office in SoHo, someone called out in my direction, "Dude!" *Huh? Is that guy talking to me?* I stopped googling "is it legal to ride a horse in New York City?" on my phone and looked up. "It IS you! You're the YouTube broker! I love your house tours and vlogs! My girlfriend and I watch them all the time." As soon as the words *Aw, thanks man!* left my mouth, I was nearly blinded by the ten-billion-watt light bulb that suddenly appeared over my head.

YOUTUBE BROKER?! OUR VIDEOS! That's it! I'm luxury real estate AND media!

We had been successfully using media to sell apartments to a wider audience for a while. In fact, I had recently sold a $40 million apartment to a man from South Africa who saw the video tour on my YouTube channel. That's a huge sale, and it came directly from social media. I had to give my team credit for pushing me in this direction. They had been encouraging me to start doing property tours, but I was skeptical. Would anyone really want to watch tours of apartments that were for sale? Their response was, people make videos to sell coffee, water, beer, makeup, clothes, jewelry . . . so why not real estate? One of our first property tours was of a $78 million mega mansion in Los Angeles. That video was watched by sixteen million people IN JUST ONE DAY. That's sooooooo many pairs of eyes. I had done three television shows on Bravo, and the exposure was incredible, but now I saw that we had the power to instantly reach nearly as many people by making our own video content. After the Los Angeles house tour made a splash, we leaned into video even more. Now we have a full-service in-house company called SERHANT. STUDIOS so we can create content that is strategically designed to resonate with the largest real estate audience in the ENTIRE WORLD. We've been successful in using multiple forms of media to sell real estate—YouTube, Instagram, television, and TikTok. These tools have become a crucial part of my success, and my use of media distinguishes me from all other brokers. I'm not just a top seller of luxury properties; I'm also the broker who can get his listings in front of The Most People. And as an added bonus, my skills from my attempted acting career all come into play here. See, Mom and Dad? That theater degree was totally worth it!

PEOPLE LOVE SHOPPING WITH FRIENDS. *BE THAT FRIEND.*

While your AND helps you differentiate yourself in your industry (so important!), it accomplishes a few other things as well. There's a good chance you've heard me say this before: "People don't like being sold to, but they love shopping with friends." Selling, at its core, is about creating a connection, not pushing a pair of plaid pants in someone's face and terrorizing them until they buy them. Whether you are selling a product or providing a service or being a thought leader, it's the AND of your brand that will create an authentic connection between you and your audience. Before Mark Manson became a best-selling author, he spent some time focusing on how he could differentiate himself as a writer while being relatable and creating a sense of trust between himself and the reader: "I was at that phase of my career where I was throwing things at a wall and seeing what stuck, and writing and blogging was what stuck. From there I needed to understand, 'Okay, who's my audience? What am I going to write about? How am I going to differentiate myself? How am I going to stand out?' Essentially all the branding questions came to the forefront. I imagine this is true of most brands, that the first thing that makes you stand out is something you don't even know you're doing—it's something that's just innately different about you. The piece of feedback I would get all the time was, 'Wow. You're so honest.' That was the starting point. I was getting into relationship advice and self-help markets, and I thought, 'A lot of these markets are bullshit. I'm just going to be honest about it.'"

Manson's blunt approach was the subtle differentiator that would have a hugely positive impact on his popularity as a writer. "Once you get into personal topics, like why you've been single for the last three years, it can be a very rough experience for a reader to have someone bluntly telling you why. So, one of the ways I started making it easier for the reader to hear was by using a lot of humor. If you can get somebody laughing, then they will be more willing to hear a difficult truth. It became a big identifying thing about my brand. It was funny, it was self-help content, but you were giggling while you read it, which people were not used to. This became the cornerstone of the Mark Manson brand, which was honest, a little bit rough around the edges, but was also funny."

In 2013, Manson's brand solidified itself as the most tell-it-like-it-is voice of self-help. "A big part of my writing was that

I wanted to write the way I talk, and I'm a foul-mouthed dude from Boston. I wrote *fuck* a lot. It showed up in my writing from day one. It wasn't calculated, but it differentiated me because it was something that was not typical in my industry. Most self-help content does not have curse words, and here's this guy cursing at you. It kind of shocks people and gets them to pay attention to you. When I put *fuck* in the title of an article for the first time it got shared like crazy. I did this a few more times, and ironically the

PRO TIP: USE THE COMPLIMENT AND CONNECT TECHNIQUE TO "BE THAT FRIEND"

I've talked about how anxious I can get in social situations, so "being that friend" is sometimes hard for me. I've devised a stress-free way of connecting with a new person (and potential source of business). While it can feel terrifying to walk up to a stranger and say, "Hi, I'm Megan," it's not scary to use the technique I call Compliment and Connect. Start with a simple compliment and use it as a gateway to conversation. "Oh, hi. Cool Braves T-shirt. Do you live in Atlanta?" People enjoy compliments, so the person you're meeting is likely to respond with a smile. "No, I live in Alabama, actually, but the Braves are my favorite team." The compliment leads to a connection, and the conversation can now focus on batting averages and RBIs, and before you know it, you'll be swapping contact info.

article 'The Subtle Art of Not Giving a F*ck' was the last article I published with the word *fuck* in it, and it just went bananas, and it eventually became the book. So, the fuck thing I accidentally fell into, but by then I did understand branding and the importance of creating an easy way for people to identify you. For better or worse, I'm the fuck guy to this day."

Your AND is also what humanizes you: it's a glimpse into *who* you are beyond *what* you do. It makes you memorable because it shows off your unique insight, talents, and curiosity and *all the things* that make you different from the woman running the competing coffee shop down the street. Trust is also a consideration here. In a time when there are many, many accessible options for *every single thing a person could ever want*—from fancy British toothpaste and cheese made by nuns to hand-knit dog sweaters and bougie candles that smell like rare flowers picked by gnomes —your AND makes an argument as to why customers should trust you, work with you, hire you, listen to you, and buy things *from you*. Your AND goes beyond the stats and figures of your business. Sharing your AND is an opportunity for you to present yourself in a way that promotes trust, connection, and authenticity. Let me show you what I'm talking about. I encourage my team members to find their AND as well, and it has served as an easy way to break the ice, connect with clients, and create a memorable brand that attracts clients like a magnet.

One of my team members knows EVERYTHING about wine. She's real estate AND wine. Give this woman a glass of red wine, and after just one sip she'll say something like, "I taste a fully sharpened number two pencil, dense black fruits that ripened under a full moon, four-leaf clovers, my grandfather's cigar . . .

and finally, just a hint of high-end denim." From rare vintages to bottles that provide a bang for your buck, she's our go-to wine expert at SERHANT. If we need to send a bottle of wine to a client, we don't do it until we ask her, and she also helps us choose the amazing wines that complement each course at our Mastermind Dinners (Join us! You'll love it!). Her passion for wine is infectious (even though my palate can't detect the flavor of sharp pencils or full-moon fruit), and she's used this knowledge as a way to create connections and boost her brand awareness. She hosts wine tastings for clients, gives the perfect bottle to new homeowners at closings, and always has interesting wines available at her open houses. She'll make property videos that show her opening a bottle of wine and talking about the properties of a specific red while simultaneously showing off the amazing chef's kitchen in the apartment she's selling. What a way to use that AND! She's great at her job, and her clients are always happy when they work with her to buy or sell a home, but you know what else they love? The emails she sends talking about her favorite vintages, the wine tasting events she cohosts with local wine stores, and the fact that a perfect wine recommendation from her is a quick text away. Her clients never have to worry about serving the wrong wine with fish! AND wine isn't just her passion and superpower . . . it's her brand, and it works.

NOW IT'S YOUR TURN

Exercise: Who Else Are You?

Finding your AND doesn't have to be as challenging as it was for me (it was right in front of me the entire time, so close I practically could have tripped over it, *and yet I did not see it*). Simply thinking about what you like to do and what you're good at outside of work will give you options *aplenty*. Answer the following questions to find your true AND:

STEP ONE: The Interest Audit

1. Let your mind wander away from work. . . . Where does it go?
2. If you were magically given two extra hours a day just for you, how would you spend them?
3. Describe a recent experience you had that was so fun it left you thinking, *Oh my God, I can't wait to do that again.*
4. Describe a recent experience where you demonstrated a skill set or bit of knowledge to someone else. How did they respond?
5. Put all concerns about practicality and earning an income aside. If you could have ANY kind of job you wanted, what would it be?
6. What are your greatest non-work-related accomplishments?

7.   What do people constantly ask you about? Recipes, your amazing shoes, where to go on vacation? I'm asked about media allllllllll the time.

STEP TWO: Identify the Commonalities

Time to check out those answers. What do you see? Look for commonalities and themes. Did you list outdoor activities? Is one of your greatest accomplishments running the New York City Marathon? You could be accounting AND hiking or gardening AND running. Maybe everything you wrote down relates to fashion or interior design. Are you queen of your book group, always offering the best recommendations? Animal lover, foodie, anglophile, film buff, yoga maven, athlete, photographer, surfer, world traveler, expert knitter? Nearly anything can be used as a tool to boost your visibility, connect with clients, and set you apart from the crowd. Write it down! Write it down NOW. Let's do this!

My commonalities are: _____

STEP THREE: Reveal Your Superpower

It's great if you're a huge reader and you're always up to date on what's new, or ready to give the perfect recommendation— but being a bibliophile won't benefit your brand unless you find ways to share it with your client base. From this moment on you are

_____ AND _____, and everything you do should be filtered through that lens. Remember that! With the possible exceptions of entomology and cage fighting, there are creative ways to wrap any AND into a brand. Remember, you're not quitting your job or going back to square one—you're infusing a part of your personality into your brand to differentiate yourself and share an interesting part of your story. When I added AND MEDIA to my brand, I used the following guidelines to make sure my superpower was coming through clearly.

Communicate: Tell your story! Get comfortable talking about your AND—share how it has impacted your life, brought you joy, or taught you new skills. You're not a blank slate anymore. Your superpower is a special part of your personality that you are sharing with clients and customers. Your AND makes you more appealing—let everyone see that! I tell all my clients, *I'll use the power of media to sell your apartment—just watch me.*

Connect: Use your AND to bring people together. Have gatherings, start a group chat, or invite people to an event. The goal is to use your AND to build bridges with potential clients and customers.

> **Learn**: Knowledge is power, especially when you can share that information in a way that's interesting to your client base. Keep people's attention by curating information, news, and ideas—be a valuable resource! Be the go-to.

One last quick tip before we wrap this up. Please be deliberate about what you share. Yes, it's great to open up a part of yourself . . . but establish limits. My AND might be MEDIA, but I'm not going to post Instagram pics of myself vegged out in front of the TV wearing a T-shirt covered in Dorito crumbs. Use common sense, please! My AND not only enhances my business by getting our properties in front of more eyes, but it is also my way of sharing more of myself with the people who trust me to sell their homes. Be the chef/personal shopper/landscaper that is so good at what they do and so interesting that clients NEED YOU IN THEIR ORBIT. Humanness has never mattered more. We need connection, we crave stories, we want to be *part of something*, and your brand will thrive by providing people with a touch of that. Be you, enjoy your AND, share it, and watch what happens when you let that positivity infuse everything you do. Trust me . . . you and your AND are going to make a helluva pair.

You've finished the next crucial part of the brand-building process! In this chapter you have accomplished the following:

Conducted an interest audit ✔
Found commonalities among your interests ✔
Identified your AND ✔

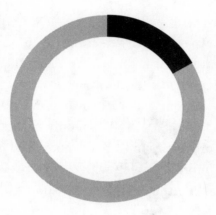

NOW IT'S SYDNEY'S TURN

INTEREST AUDIT

1. **Let your mind wander away from work. . . . Where does it go?**
   The gym, family time, my own processes I'd like to optimize for productivity, organizing my apartment, cleaning . . . hyperactive brain at the LEAST.

2. **If you were magically given two extra hours a day just for you, how would you spend them?**
   Reading or learning a new skill.

3. **Describe a recent experience you had that was so fun it left you thinking, *Oh my God, I can't wait to do that again.***
   Competing in my first Hyrox race! It's a hybrid race that combines endurance and strength exercises, all done for time. It was easily the HARDEST thing I've ever done, but one of my favorite moments. Seeing my family cheer for me on the sidelines made me so happy, and crossing that finish line made all the hard work worth it! I'm already training for another one.

4. **Describe a recent experience where you demonstrated a skill set or bit of knowledge to someone else. How did they respond?**
   I consulted a friend on a few ways she could improve her lead pipeline to reach more personal training

clients. She was grateful and kept saying, "Wow! You're so smart!" It always feels good to help fellow small business owners build out the processes they need to scale their businesses.

5. **Put all concerns about practicality and earning an income aside. If you could have ANY kind of job you wanted, what would it be?**

   I LOVE all my work, and I love doing a little bit of everything. If I had twenty-four hours in a day to do whatever I wanted . . . I'd spend it coaching, doing my own training, helping other small business owners build their businesses, and of course, catching up on *The Bachelor*.

6. **What are your greatest non-work-related accomplishments?**

   My favorite accomplishment has been building my life here in New York. It's been challenging, it's been scary, but there's nothing more rewarding than coming home to my apartment at the end of a long day and realizing that THIS is my life.

7. **What do people constantly ask you about? Recipes, your amazing shoes, where to go on vacation?**

   a. The best workouts
   b. The best Trader Joe's snacks (I'm a BIG Trader Joe's girl)
   c. If XYZ is "healthy"
   d. Marketing and community-building questions
   e. What it's like to work for Ryan Serhant :)

Commonalities

I love learning new things, using my business skills to help other trainers, a variety of interests. My best accomplishments come from areas beyond training.

My AND

I am a fitness coach AND a busy, thriving professional.

Thoughts from Sydney

For me, this felt important to convey because making time for your mental and physical well-being can feel like a CHORE when you're already so busy with work, trying to maintain a social life, taking care of your friends and family, etc. I feel that leaning into my other projects in addition to fitness makes it feel more attainable to find a routine that works well for my individual needs and capabilities.

CHAPTER 5

How to Be the One:
Finding Your Brand Personality

People form connections with other people, not companies. That's why it's actually *the personification* of a brand that catches our attention and draws us in. Let's think of it this way: You've been in a wonderful relationship for a couple of years, and now you are ready for the next BIG step. You plan to take your partner on a romantic getaway to the beach. At sunset, with the dolphins frolicking in the sea as your witnesses, you're going to present your beloved with champagne, flowers, and ta-da . . . an engagement ring! You've found the person (hardest part!), booked the plane tickets, made hotel reservations, and bought a new swimsuit. The only thing that's left to do is acquire THE RING. You get right to work, researching your options. *Okay, so there's the Fictional Diamond Company, and they look pretty good. I wonder who's on the board of directors there these days. Oh, nice—according to industry reports their revenues are growing! Let's see if I can find information on their cash balance. Well, their debt ratio seems fine, and their expenses are flat. Looks like there's a solid return on their equity too. Great! The Fictional Diamond Company it is!* Now that you've researched this company like you're conducting a valuation

93

before an IPO, you can march into this imaginary store and plop down a large sum of money on the ring you will present to your beloved at a five-star resort. Oh, you made sure to look up that resort on the S&P 500 before making that reservation, right?

WRONG WRONG WRONG WRONG WRONG and WRONG.

Maybe this is how robots shop, but this is not generally how humans make decisions about what they buy. Sure, there are many purchases where we factor in cost and the reputation of who we're buying from, but there is a deeper reason that influences our choices. Whether you decide to buy a ring from Tiffany & Co. or from a local jeweler isn't about balance sheets and stock prices. What really drives us to select a specific brand is that brand's personality. **A brand personality is a powerful combination of humanistic qualities that creates an emotional and/or intellectual response in the consumer.** Brand personality impacts our decision-making when it comes to buying nearly everything—pens, coffee, socks, clothes, shoes, food, and paper towels. If you're thinking, *Ryan, paper towels don't have any personality*, I'm here to tell you you're wrong. Brand personality *always* plays a role, whether you're aware of it or not (look at that pun, nice!). You might find that writing with a particular brand of pen is so enjoyable you'd prefer to chisel notes on a stone tablet rather than touch any other brand of pen. Your favorite pen writes smoothly, is dependable, and looks cute in your hand as you sit in the local coffee shop writing down all your brilliant ideas. You love it so much that ALL other brands of pen are dead to you. As for those boring, lifeless paper towels you automatically throw in your grocery cart every single time you go to the store? Maybe it's because subconsciously you know that Paper Towel X's brand personality of "dependable, durable, and absorbent" is exactly what you need to clean up the puddles of pee your new puppy leaves on the kitchen floor. And what about that diamond ring burning a hole in your pocket? You either bought it from Tiffany & Co. because you were drawn to their brand personality that exudes sophistication, quality, timelessness, and elegance . . . or you went with a local jeweler whose brand encompasses service, trustworthiness, and value. We are all drawn to these relatable characteristics when we're making choices about brands. *A pen is never just a pen—it's an instrument for self-expression! A ring is more than jewelry—it is symbolic of a lifetime commitment! I watch the news on channel XYZ in the morning because I like getting my news from their anchor person more than anyone else!* That's why one of the most important things you can do for your personal brand is home in on its true personality before you share it with the rest of the world. Nik Sharma, CEO of Sharma Brands, believes understanding a brand's personality is so important that the company imagines brands are actual people: "When building a brand, the brand itself needs to be clearly defined in terms of who they are. There's an exercise we always do. If this brand was a person, who are they? Who are their friends? Where do they eat? What are they doing on a Friday night . . . staying home and cooking, ordering in? What does this brand like to share on Instagram? What are they retweeting? I think it comes down to defining what this brand is as a living being, which it is, kind of, and then figuring out how to apply that to content."

Brand personality is the lifeblood of your brand. All the feelings you want people to have when they encounter you, your service, or your product start right here. Happy, comforted, relieved, energized, sophisticated, luxurious, tough, dependable. . . . Whatever feeling you're going for, all this needs to be channeled through your brand's personality. This is about taking the spirit of your brand and ensuring it shines through *everything* you do. Highlighting brand personality lets people see beyond your brand's face value so they can form an emotional connection. The goal of that connection is for your brand to be the number one go-to brand no matter what it is you do. The VERY second someone thinks, *I need to redecorate, work with a new SEO company, hire someone to walk the dog, buy a new car, replace this power drill, organize these photographs—anything,* suddenly an ultra-positive image of your brand pops up in their head like magic. Customers don't even need to THINK about who to call, what website to order from, or what store to walk into because they know that YOUR BRAND is exactly what they need right now. While I was building my brand, I knew that I wanted people seeking luxury properties to think, *Oh, I know who to call! SERHANT.* Period. End of story. There were a few specific steps I took to ensure my brand personality would pop into my audience's head. I made sure my brand personality had ESP.

TO MAKE YOUR BRAND THE ONE, USE ESP

1. Emphasize the brand image

When you think of Ford trucks and their tagline, *Built Ford tough,* you don't just think, *Truck. Right. Those are the vehicles that are larger than cars but still have four wheels.* Those three little words—*built Ford tough*—were carefully curated to paint a specific picture. They are practically inserting an image directly into your head—rugged, dependable, hardworking, proud, uniquely American. The job of the adjectives used to describe a brand personality is to take an object and transform it into *an object with a story.* There are lots of different vehicles, but a Ford truck is the one for hauling around big, heavy objects and driving through difficult terrain like it's no big deal. *Mud? Whatever. Quicksand? Mere child's play.* Then there's all that wood you just chopped down in the forest that you need to take home to your log cabin. What are you going to do? Transport a cord of wood in a prissy little sedan like the one Grandma drives to church? No way! Your rugged, tough, and earthy lifestyle requires a truck . . . a Ford truck. The brand personality emphasizes all of the brand's core qualities, helping to form a very specific image in the mind of the consumer.

2. Speak to the customer you want

A brand's personality is like an ultra-powerful magnet that can be used to pull a specific audience directly to your brand. The human characteristics a brand exudes will speak to like-minded people who are interested in the overall experience your brand has to offer—not just the product itself. Think of Mercedes and their tag line: *The best or nothing.* The best? OR NOTHING!? Seriously? Like we'll just Uber or walk wherever we're going? Mercedes is not messing around. That phrase, *the best or nothing,* conjures up words like *exclusivity, selective, quality, high-end, elegance, craftsmanship,* and *sophistication.* Mercedes is sending a direct signal to *a select group* of potential car owners that their brand is not your average, everyday car. We all know that any car can get you from point A to point B, but that's irrelevant here. The words they are using to describe their brand personality speak directly to the consumer they are targeting. This car is a luxury that not everyone can afford to drive. If you want to increase your status (and smell expensive leather every time you open your car door), a Mercedes is the car for you.

3. Perfect your voice

The ideal adjectives to describe a brand's personality will set the groundwork for the tone and voice you use every time you communicate with your audience (and stay tuned for the deep dive into communication in part 2). Think of communicating your brand's personality the way an ambassador might represent their nation. There's a precise tone and voice used to convey the personality of the United States accurately. Imagine the US ambassador to France showing up at the French embassy wearing a Megadeth T-shirt, shorts, and flip-flops, shouting, *Dudes! You guys want to hang out? Paris is AWESOME, so let's blow this embassy and hit up a café where we can drink wine and eat frites while chain-smoking cigarettes. Man. It's so cool that you can smoke in public here.* At your typical college frat house, this would all be A-okay. But in this case, the voice and tone in this situation would be considered rude, vulgar, and embarrassing. Not at all the right tone for a nation that is generally associated with freedom, strength, and power. Everything your brand communicates must be an extension of its personality; every engagement must promote those core emotions you want your customers to experience. Voice and tone are a crucial layer when you share your brand with the world. By perfecting your voice, you are establishing a form of communication with your customers that allows them to feel like they personally know your brand, making it more likely for them to buy your product or use your service.

FIND YOUR POWER ADJECTIVES

Let's be honest, talking about adjectives sounds about as exciting as watching paint dry. Don't worry, this isn't a grammar lesson. We are going to find three words that describe your brand's personality and use them to create a mental picture of your brand, connect with your audience, and establish the mood or feeling you want to convey. Words have power. *Wait, what? Your fiancé-to-be ran off with a yoga instructor before your fancy engagement vacation and you're single again and ready for online dating?* So, what do you think would happen if this was your online dating profile?

```
Live human seeks other human (also alive)
for some kind of relationship. I am
medium height, normal weight, I eat food,
sleep in an apartment, and have a job.
```

The answer is you would be alone FOREVER. The most desperate person on earth wouldn't respond to that profile. There are no words in that description that spark any curiosity whatsoever. It gives no insight into who this person is or what appealing qualities they might have. It's also impossible to glean anything about this person's character. The only mental picture we can create based on that description is this person is ALIVE. That's a very low bar. This might be a ridiculous dating profile, but I can't tell you how many times I've encountered real estate brokers that describe themselves with zero-added-value words.

You're "hardworking and dependable"? *Oh my God, where have you been all my life? The only applicants I ever get are "lazy losers who show up 50 percent of the time."* Aren't qualities like "hardworking" and "dependable" a given no matter what industry you work in? You've got to have high expectations for yourself if you want people to have high expectations of your brand. Taking the time to discover the best adjectives for your brand will elevate it to a new level. Stick with zero-added-value adjectives and watch your brand fade into the background like a boring dating profile. Ultimately, we're asking a lot of the words that will define your brand's personality—so carefully choose power adjectives that will make your star rise. Words have power.

Power Adjective Guidelines

Before we start unearthing your adjectives, let me share the guidelines I followed while I was working on my power adjectives:

1. **No zero-added-value words.** You heard me, but I'll say it again. No low-hanging fruit, please. Basic descriptive words like *dependable, hardworking,* and *honest* are OUT. I mean, c'mon! Seriously, those are baseline qualities, and we're looking for words that make your brand stand out. Remember to think big and have high expectations for your brand. If you choose words that easily describe *every single person in the world* who does what you do, it's not good enough.

2. **Stick with your story.** Since my brand is luxury real estate AND media, I needed to find adjectives that express that specific idea. Focus is key here, and make sure your adjectives describe both what you do as well as your AND—but stop there. I think of myself as an imaginative and creative person, but that doesn't fit in with the main objective of my brand. Creativity is more of a side story. The word *creative* doesn't explain why I'm the best person to call when you want to find a penthouse in Tribeca, so it's not a front-facing part of my brand personality. Your power adjectives need to directly and clearly relate to your brand's main objective to make the biggest impact.

3. **Support your core values.** Remember! People connect with other people, not with companies, and you strengthen that connection by being consistent (we'll get WAY into that soon). The words you choose to describe your brand personality cannot conflict with your core values. Since one of our treasured values at SERHANT. is *future-driven*, we would never refer to ourselves as *old-fashioned* or *traditional*. Not that there's anything wrong with those words! They just don't match our values. Using adjectives that conflict with your core values makes you look like a confused mess, and who wants to hire those people who don't seem to have *any idea* what they're talking about? No one does. That's why you need to choose a power adjective that gives potential customers a glimpse of what the brand stands for. This is another way you will strengthen your connection to your target audience.

Without further ado (wow, I've never had an opportunity to say that in my entire life), my power adjectives are

successful, limitless, polished.

I chose these words because they are an accurate reflection of my brand and what I stand for. I'm emphasizing *successful* because I want to highlight my actual experience selling luxury apartments. I don't just galivant around Manhattan with a set of keys opening doors for people—monkeys can do that. I *sell*. I'm a closer. I have an unbeatable track record. Bottom line, you want to sell your $90 million penthouse or a $125 million beachfront mansion? Hire the broker who is successful AF (you understand I'm referring to myself here, right?).

Limitless provides a peek into my personal philosophy and core values. You've probably heard me say "Expansion always, in all ways." I believe this with every fiber of my six-foot-three being. No matter what the situation—the penthouse you love has an unlucky apartment number and you'll be cursed forever if it isn't changed, you want permission from the co-op board to live with your pet kangaroo, you can't possibly close on the apartment unless you can be sure it isn't haunted, so your poltergeist consultant needs immediate access—I WILL find a solution. *Limitless* encompasses my work ethic (unstoppable), my scope for my business (huge), and what I'll do to find or sell a property (anything that's not considered a felony).

Polished is also a multifaceted power adjective. I am literally polished. I am not the kind of broker who is going to show up unshaven and in a sweatshirt, even if it's a weekend. True story: I was once run over by a caffeine-crazed maniac as I was entering a

Starbucks. I sprained my ankle badly and ended up in an air cast. I was very close to selling an apartment at 230 West Fifty-Sixth Street to a couple who had been looking for months. So, when they called on a Saturday to say they needed to look at it *one more time even though I had showed it to them again YESTERDAY*, I stuffed my giant balloon leg into a suit and hobbled to the subway on crutches (this was pre-Yuriy). Even if I'm physically maimed, I'm polished. Suit. Tie. Shoes (so shiny they are blinding). *Polished* has another meaning. I do whatever I can to make sure every aspect of the transaction runs smoothly. Communication, negotiation, paperwork, showings, EVERYTHING. I'll never forget the look on the buyers' faces when I showed up. It was a combination of surprise (I'd had two working legs when they saw me yesterday) and *wow, you don't mess around when it comes to selling real estate.* I had worked too hard to let a stupid balloon cast keep me from being the embodiment of successful, limitless, and polished. My leg healed, and that couple bought the apartment for $8 million.

All three of my power adjectives fit in with my AND as well. I have a proven record of *success* on TV—ten years of *Million Dollar Listing New York, Ryan's Wedding, Ryan's Renovation*, and *Sell It Like Serhant*, plus thousands of videos we've made that have garnered millions of views. *Limitless* definitely describes my amazing team at SERHANT. Studios. My team is top-notch and can do anything. Drone flying over the East River to get the best shot? Fine. A marketing video that's inspired by French black-and-white art house films? *Let's go.* My team is also up to date on all the new developments with different social media platforms. Finally, *polished*. People in the media do not look like slobs. No news anchor has sat behind that desk wearing their pajamas and yawning as they report on the latest developments in Washington, DC. People in media are polished! See? All three of my adjectives provide extra support to my AND.

HERE ARE A FEW POWER ADJECTIVES TO GET YOU STARTED

Influential, unstoppable, dynamic, electrifying, outstanding, substantial, successful, flawless, first-rate, phenomenal, exemplary, exceptional, top-notch, remarkable, creative, imaginative, unique, sublime, supreme, unrivaled, superb, masterful, unparalleled, passionate, inspiring, uplifting, vibrant, brilliant, insightful, intuitive, savvy, erudite, perceptive, astute, sharp, clever, gritty, iron-willed, unyielding, relentless, tireless, unshakable, steadfast, curious, unbeatable, graceful, elegant, chic.

That should get you going. I'd love to hear any interesting adjectives you come up with! Email me at ryan@serhant.com.

NOW IT'S YOUR TURN

Exercise: Uncover Your True Brand Personality

STEP ONE: *How do you see yourself?*

Today, right now, at this very moment, who are you? You're going to set a timer for fifteen minutes, and during that time you're going to write down adjectives about YOURSELF. Don't freak out about the guidelines I set earlier because we'll refine these later. Don't be shy or modest, and do not overthink this. Just write down a big list of adjectives that describe YOU. GO!

STEP TWO: *How do others see you?*

You got the ball rolling with that first exercise—well done, and we'll refer to that list soon. Now we're going to get a little more specific. The next exercises will focus on how you're viewed by others.

1. The following is a list of people you likely interact with on the regular. Answer each question, but with THREE words. ONLY three—we're narrowing things down here!
    How would fellow team members describe you?
    How would clients describe you?
    Why would clients refer you to other people?
2. Collect any client testimonials in one place. Get out your favorite highlighter (mine is blue, of course) and

go to work highlighting any adjective that's been used to describe you.

3.   BONUS BRANDING CHALLENGE: If you're willing to take this process further, you can! Prepare three emails to colleagues and three emails to current or former clients. We've included templates at the end of this chapter to help you craft your letters. The basic idea here is to connect with clients and colleagues and explain that you're working on your personal branding. Ask them if they'd be open to giving you three adjectives that describe your personality so that you can understand more about how your business is currently perceived. If you think this feels weird, know that many people who have taken my masterclass and done this have found that the people they've contacted have been very flattered! Do it!

STEP THREE: Reconcile and refine

1.   **Locate the zone of authenticity.** Now that you have a bunch of lists and highlighted papers in front of you, we can dive in. Make a list (yes, another one—I swear we are almost finished) of any overlap between your list of adjectives and the words you've collected from other people. You want to include any direct matches as well as words that are similar in meaning. You wrote down *breathtaking*, and your client used the word *showstopping* to describe your

floral design company? Write those down, but feel free to choose the one you think has the best ring to it. The words you've written down that correlate to what others have said, behold! This is your ZONE OF AUTHENTICITY. It's that sweet spot where what you think and what people think *of you* meet. THIS IS WHO YOU ARE! These words are the best potential candidates for your power adjectives.

2. **Check that AND!** Remember, at least one of the adjectives on your list of candidates should correlate to your AND. This word should align naturally with your AND as well as provide your customers with a hint of what you do beyond the main purpose of your brand.

3. **Test out those power adjectives.** Write down the three power adjectives you've curated from the steps above. You might be over the moon about what you've discovered. YOU'VE NAILED IT! Or maybe you're feeling, *Wait, am I really* edgy, innovative, *and* perceptive? You're not getting this tattooed on your chest (not yet, anyway). Try them out; sit with them. Let these adjectives sink in, and allow yourself to get used to them! They likely *do* represent you and your brand's personality very well. It's not every day we boil down the essence of our true personality to just three words. Give it a minute! You've got this!

Remember, while power adjectives are IMPORTANT, there's no right or wrong answers here. There will be no quizzes. No one will receive a prize (your brand ruling the universe is the prize). Ultimately, this is about what feels right to you. It's about which words motivate you to get wildly excited about taking your brand to the next level. There is no rule that says people who sell high-end real estate need to be *polished*—that's my authentic take on my brand. You could be high-end real estate AND sailing, meeting clients at mansions sporting a tan and wind-swept hair. What works for you doesn't necessarily work for other people doing something similar, and isn't that the entire point? These words are impacted by your take on them, and there are so many valid plays when it comes to finding adjectives to describe your brand personality. So, bottom line—the words need to feel right to you, because they are going to be the lens through which everything about your brand is examined. If you look at any touch point for me on social media, you'll see EVERY single post is filtered through my power adjectives. I literally stop, take a moment, and ask myself, Do this photo and caption represent *successful, limitless*, and *polished*? If yes, then READY, SET, GO! If not, DELETE. New photo, please!

Troubleshooting: *Hmmmm. Ryan, none of my adjectives align perfectly with my AND. Help!*

Solution: Put yourself in their shoes.

Don't freak out. Let's talk this through. Focus directly on your AND for a few minutes. If you are real estate AND the expert for finding homes for large families, and so far your words are *unstoppable, savvy*, and *integrity*, ask yourself what's missing. Imagine YOU are your ideal customer. What adjective would you use to describe the person you want to hire? What would you be looking for in a person to help you find a home for your family of eight? I imagine you'd want someone who is *warm, wholesome,* or *family focused.*

SOMETIMES PERSONALITIES ARE TERRIBLE

When it comes to branding, things have personalities too . . . and sometimes they are terrible. While you can make it your mission to be as *on brand* as possible, there are occasionally things that are not within our control. Not too long ago, I was about to sell a $10 million apartment in lower Manhattan to a couple named Mai and Henry. We had been looking at apartments forever, and they finally found "the one." Just as we were about to sign the contract, I got a frantic phone call: "Ryan. It turns out we cannot buy this apartment. The number of the apartment is 44." I had no idea what she was talking about . . . then she explained that the number 44 is to be avoided at all costs in her culture. In Mandarin, "four four" is pronounced like "*sz sz,*" which means DIE DIE. "Ryan, I cannot call my mother and tell her I just bought a double death apartment."

Just when I think I've encountered every problem—a co-op board that won't accept a kangaroo (it was small!), a client who didn't show up for his closing (he was in jail)—the universe tosses me a fresh dose of hell in the form of an insane problem. "Okay, so you still love the apartment, but it can't be apartment 44?"

I heard an exasperated sigh on the other end of the phone, like I had just suggested she move into the tiger habitat at the Bronx Zoo. "We are not buying the double death apartment, Ryan! Would you want every package you receive to say DIE DIE on it?"

I knew the other penthouses had sold, so there was no chance of buying an apartment with a nice number like 42 or 43. "So, if I could get rid of the number 44, you would still buy it?"

Another sigh. "Of course we would, Ryan!"

I started flipping through my mental Rolodex of penthouses for sale in lower Manhattan. I knew that none of the other apartments were going to work for them, and I knew I wouldn't be able to convince them to look at a different neighborhood. I wanted to scream, cry, and eat ice cream all at the same time. As I was thinking about the closest place to grab some cookies and cream, something occurred to me. I couldn't change the fact that the developer numbered their penthouse 44, or that my buyers came from a culture where that number is to be avoided at all costs, but I could rebrand the apartment so it was no longer associated with death! Changing the number of the apartment was harder than I thought it would be. It involved another negotiation with the seller, filling out forms, calling the city, informing the fire department and the police . . . but we made it happen. When Mai and Henry signed their contract, it specifically stated that under no circumstances would their apartment be numbered 44. It would be labeled penthouse A.

This experience taught me that when you face an obstacle that isn't within your control, sometimes the easiest solution is right in front of you . . . with a minor rebrand. If I hadn't been able to change that number, the entire process would have started all over again. Instead, this tiny brand personality tweak meant that I sold an apartment, the developer was happy, and Mai and Henry were comfortably settled in their completely death-free apartment. Before you start from scratch on a project or start desperately throwing solutions against a wall, hoping something will stick, ask yourself if a tiny rebrand is the solution.

What's so great about this part of the branding process is that you're essentially designing a living, breathing entity that encompasses all your dreams, ambitions, and goals. You are taking your job, dressing it up in all its finery, and introducing it, fully formed, to the rest of the world. Defining your power adjectives is about taking control—it's about knowing you have something remarkable to share and *sharing it*. For years I was Ryan Serhant, tough negotiator, reality show broker, a.k.a. the gray-haired one who does some goofy stuff on TV and sells tons of apartments. You know what? It was great, but now I know there's more. Now that I'm Ryan Serhant, CEO of SERHANT., who is successful, limitless, and polished, it's like I've launched myself into the stratosphere. It's next level. The work I've done to refine and enhance what's best about my brand has cemented my place as the go-to broker for luxury apartments, and business has skyrocketed. I'm not working longer hours, and I haven't cloned myself so that I can be in two places at once—I've simply chiseled out who I really am, and I'm crystal clear on what I have to offer. Creating your personal brand is like building your very own stairway to the stars. The stairway is paved with your dreams and goals, and you have those three powerful adjectives supporting you during your ascent. Now, let's see how high you can climb.

BONUS EXERCISES

Reach out to past clients and current colleagues to help with this assignment. I've included two sample emails that I have encouraged my team to use. These emails are great starting points, but be sure to personalize them for each person you send them to.

Colleague Email

Hi NAME:

Start with a brief personal but complimentary greeting that pertains to your industry.

For example, Congratulations on winning first place in the pie-eating contest!

OR

It was great to see you at the annual competitive eaters' convention. Your advice about how to swallow hot dog buns whole made a real impact on me.

I just read the book *Brand It Like Serhant: How to Stand Out from the Crowd, Build Your Following, and Earn More Money*. I'm currently working on defining my brand personality, and I'd appreciate it if you'd take a moment to answer one question. What three words would you use to describe my personality?

Wrap up with a personalized ending.

Thank you so much for helping! It would be great to treat you to a glass of wine. Any chance that you are available next week?

Sincerely,

Your name

Past Client Email

Dear NAME:

Start with a brief remark that will remind them of the work you did together.

For example, How have you been? I haven't seen you since your kitchen renovation was finished, and I hope you're enjoying your new space. I think the tiles we picked out together were absolutely perfect!

I am currently working on developing and refining my personal brand. As a past client, your input and feedback are important, and I'd be grateful if you could answer one quick question that will help me with the endeavor. If you were to recommend my services to someone in your network, what three words would you use to describe my personality?

Wrap up with an offer (it doesn't have to be big) to show you appreciate their attention, such as:

As a thank you, I'd love to treat you to a coffee. Are you available next Thursday?

I also attached a review for a new restaurant that opened near your office. I know you love sushi, so I wanted to make sure you saw it!

I drank the most wonderful merlot last night, and I want to bring you a bottle. I'll be in your neighborhood Saturday, and I can drop it off.

Sincerely,

Your name

Current Client Email—send this only to a client who has a signed contract and actually knows you!

Dear Client's Name:

Start with a positive, light reference to your current business with them.

For example, Your daughter's bridal shower went off so beautifully! I am so glad my catering was a hit. I'm also very excited about catering your husband's fiftieth birthday next month.

I am currently working on developing and refining my personal brand. I deeply respect your input and feedback as a client and would be grateful if you could answer one quick question that will help with the endeavor. If you were to recommend my services to someone in your network, what three words would you use to describe my personality?

Wrap up with a small offer.

For example, Thank you so much for assisting me with this. I just refined a new blueberry muffin recipe! I'd love to bring some by for you to sample!

Sincerely,

Your name

You are well on your way to fully understanding your core identity. In this chapter you have accomplished the following:

Used ESP to:

Emphasize your brand image ✔
Speak to the customer you want ✔
Perfect your voice ✔

Discovered your power adjectives ✔

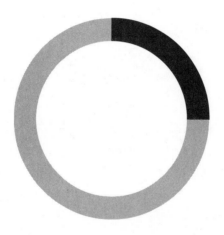

NOW IT'S SYDNEY'S TURN

MY ADJECTIVES

1. Strong
2. Supportive
3. Empowering
4. Confident
5. Empathetic
6. Intelligent
7. Successful
8. Driven

HOW DO OTHERS SEE YOU?

How would colleagues or team members describe you?

1. Curious and willing to learn and improve
2. Aspirational but driven by short-term goals
3. Lighthearted and supportive

How would clients describe you?

1. Motivating but not pushy
2. Eager to celebrate small wins
3. Someone who believes in your potential

Why would clients refer you to other people?

1. I prioritize educating my clients so they can set and achieve their wellness goals independently

2. I encourage clients to challenge their limiting beliefs and surprise themselves

MY BRAND PERSONALITY IS:

1. Empowering
2. Educational
3. Supportive

CHAPTER 6

Creating Your Visual Identity the Right Way

A strong visual identity unleashes a brand's true power, providing a way for people to connect and interact with it. Visual identity is also why none of us have trouble locating our go-to toothpaste, soap, or shampoo—its design, color scheme, and logo are practically burned into our brains. A brand's visual identity is created to ensure that a person who has been using toothpaste X for decades doesn't stop mid-toothbrushing and realize, *Oops. It looks like I accidentally bought Toothpaste Y. Hmmm, I've been using Toothpaste X since the moment I got teeth, but it turns out that Toothpaste Y is just as minty fresh, so from now on I guess I'll just buy whatever.* This is why **visual identity, or the carefully crafted visual expression of your brand's story, including (but not limited to) typography, logo, graphics, headshots, and lifestyle photography,** is so important! Think of it as your brand springing to life after all that careful planning! Creating your visual identity is a fun and exciting part of this process, but I have to be honest with you. The first time I took a stab at building a personal brand I made the same mistake so many other people make. I jumped headfirst into colors and fonts. So many great options! So fun! I thought that coming up with a great logo and choosing a color scheme was the same as building a brand. It's not.

In 2010, I had been selling real estate for a couple of years, dutifully toiling away in my office above Burger Heaven on Forty-Ninth Street and Madison. I noticed that there were a few brokers who were incredibly successful, and in my mind their brands were *huge*. There was "the townhouse king of the Upper West Side." This guy wasn't flashy (despite the name, there were no crowns, fur-trimmed cloaks, or footmen catering to his every whim), and he didn't have a big team, just one assistant. But everyone knew he was The Man when it came to selling townhouses on the Upper West Side of Manhattan. *Your client wants a twenty-foot-wide move-in-ready townhouse a block away from Central Park that has a chef's kitchen, a cellar that will hold an extensive wine collection, and enough room for a chicken coop in the backyard? What are you waiting for? Call The Townhouse King!*

The THKOTUWS wasn't the only broker in town who had a clear purpose and identity. There was the I-sell-lofts-in-SoHo-and-drive-a-Bentley broker. There was a broker who specialized in Upper East Side penthouses. You could spot her from blocks away because she always had a crazy scarf around her neck. There was Madame Classic Six. She sold gorgeous, sprawling old-school apartments and conducted all her business from a table at the restaurant of the Plaza Hotel. Finally, there was the broker who was obsessed with opera. He had season tickets to the New York Metropolitan Opera, and during intermission he would walk around the lobby with a glass of champagne, chatting up the uber wealthy and collecting new clients. It's the opera—it's long.

That means there are multiple intermissions. Opera man was closing deals left and right, all while just enjoying his life. I realized that these brokers weren't just crushing it; they were memorable. I had to wonder, was there anything memorable about me I could use to draw more attention and business to myself?

This question was eating at me like a garra rufa* with a pair of fresh feet . . . nibbling away at my soul, bit by tiny bit. I didn't have season tickets to anything, and I hadn't worn any statement-making outfits since I gave up my Hawaiian shirt collection in high school. *Why would anyone call me, Mr. Invisible, when they can just talk to opera broker about their dream apartment between bites of caviar blinis? Face it, Ryan, you're just a random broker in a sea of thousands who works above a hamburger shop and rides around town on a purple Vespa. Hmmm. Vespa. Purple. Wait a minute, that's it!* And that is how I ended up with my first brand attempt, which was

PURPLE.

I was really into purple back then. Aside from the purple Vespa, I slept each night in the bedroom I had also painted a bright shade of purple. It's not like I wore purple every day, but I had a decent-size collection of purple T-shirts, gym shorts, ties, and socks too. My thinking was, *Purple is my spirit color and therefore my brand!* What I didn't know then is that designing your brand around your favorite color isn't building a brand . . .

---

* Garra rufa are the fish used in a particular kind of Japanese pedicure where the fish gnaw off your dead skin. I felt like I was being slowly but surely consumed by this puzzle of a question.

that's coming up with a theme for a tween's birthday party. Since I had nailed down a color, I went ahead and chose a font that I liked. Standard fonts like Roman and Garamond were too basic for me. Instead, I went with the very lush and expensive-sounding Caviar Dreams. Nothing says "Call me! I'll sell your apartment for a record-breaking price!" like a font named after fish roe from the Acipenseridae family. I didn't stop there. I decided to distinguish myself even further. I used all lowercase letters in my name because *none* of the other brokers did that. (Hmm, wonder why. Maybe because it looks ridiculous?) I was really on a roll, so next I had a logo designed for my team THAT DID NOT YET EXIST. So, essentially, I was the purple-fish-egg-all-lowercase-letters-broker-who-worked-with-an-invisible-team guy.

In retrospect, I appreciate my forward thinking—imagining my future self working with a team under a solid brand that I had built. Unfortunately, I went about branding completely the wrong way and made my choices for all the wrong reasons. Unlike you, who are doing this *the right way*, I did zero work on my core identity. I had no brand vision, no AND, no sense of my brand personality, no adjectives. All I had was a burning desire to sell real estate and a deep love of all things purple. I didn't truly know who I was or what I had to offer, which is how I ended up with a brightly colored pseudo-brand that didn't launch me anywhere near the stratosphere. My purple brand was meh. It didn't necessarily do any harm, but it did nothing to help me generate more business, and *isn't that the point?* Thankfully, purple Ryan (and the Vespa) are in my past, I've built a brand that truly reflects who I am, and my business is thriving as a result. As we take this next big step and start exploring options for your visual identity, please keep the following in mind.

VISUAL BRANDING THE SERHANT. WAY

1. Your visual identity is NOT about personal style

Visual identity is *an expression* of your brand personality, not just a showcase of your own personal style. I can't stress enough that your visual identity isn't a decoration, and it's not something that should be based on *how you feel*. You might love florals and leopard print (who doesn't?), but that doesn't mean that wild patterns have a place in the visual identity of your law firm. While creating your visual identity requires good design, it is design *with purpose*. The adjectives you came up with in the previous chapter will serve as your guide. Your adjectives are *strategic, forward-thinking*, and *cutting-edge*? Great, and that's also exactly why you need to forget about that adorable cartoon drawing of a bunny because it is NOT going to send the right message (unless you change direction and open a pet store). Please, take a lesson from purple Ryan and look beyond what you personally find appealing. Bottom line? The visual identity of your brand needs to complement your brand adjectives—otherwise you'll have a mixed-up brand that's not going to launch you across the street much less into the stratosphere where the big money is made.

2. Great design can't fix a shaky core identity

Purple did nothing for me because other than the socks I was wearing, purple didn't connect with who I was or how I wanted to be perceived in my industry. Unless I was planning to buy a vineyard and start producing red wine (grapes are purple!), purple wasn't going to help me reach any of my goals. Visual identity is like the perfect icing on the carefully crafted cake that represents you. If your cake looks like it was made by a three-year-old and tastes like a dirty shoe, there is no frosting in the world that can make it better. The cake, a.k.a. your personal brand, can't be solely dependent on the frosting (yes, by frosting I mean your visual identity) to make it great. Don't even think of frosting that cake until you know that cake is *frosting-worthy*. So, take a minute. Before diving into your visual identity, give yourself a quick sanity check. Do your brand vision, your AND, and your brand personality and adjectives feel right to you? Are you ready to frost this thing and start serving it up to the rest of humanity? Or do you need to tweak the recipe first? If you're ready for the next big step—that is, fonts, colors, and logos—great. If you need to make sure your recipe truly works before you start slicing it up, that's okay. Just pause. Let yourself sit with what you've created. Maybe you're ready to move forward, or maybe you need to tweak that recipe slightly. If you need to adjust your recipe, now is the time to do it, because it is nearly impossible to unfrost a cake!

3. Fun follows foundation

You've probably heard the phrase *form follows function*. It was coined by the architect Louis H. Sullivan, who is known as the father of the high-rise. What he meant by that is an object's shape and design should mostly relate to its purpose. For example, when you walk into the restaurant Cipriani Wall Street, which is located in a Greek revival building (modeled off the Pantheon in Rome) that formerly housed the headquarters for National City Bank (now Citibank), you can't help but be amazed by the splendor. I swear you can smell the money even though it hasn't been a bank in decades. The massive dining room features a dome that soars seventy feet into the air, and it is decorated so elegantly I wouldn't have been surprised if someone had said to me, "Sorry, sir. This restaurant is for royalty only. I'm afraid if you don't have your crown and scepter with you, you'll have to eat elsewhere." Everything about the place, from the perfectly set tables to the chic, impeccably dressed customers, practically shouts *Eating here is going to cost you a ton of money, and it will be worth it.* However, if you are starving and seeking a quick and less bank-breaking culinary experience, your typical diner with its more utilitarian and basic design suggests that anyone is welcome, and if it's disco fries you're after, just take a seat and you'll be dipping fries in gravy within minutes.

Any visuals you select must suit the purpose of your business. If you own a high-end clothing boutique, clients need to know what they're in for the second they step into the store. If you're selling vicuña sweaters for thousands of dollars, everything about the space, from the color scheme to the way you display your wares, needs to support the idea that your establishment is ultra-elite. In other words, if your store is as bright and busy as your typical Walmart, your intended customer is not going to feel inspired to plunk down a pile of cash for a luxurious sweater. We all know that Walmart is the kind of place that carries all the basics of life. This is immediately clear when you walk into the store and see the never-ending aisles that contain everything from boxes of cereal to laundry detergent. When it comes to creating a visual identity, it is foundation first. Your visuals must support your purpose so that they accurately express your adjectives and brand personality (everything goes back to your core identity!).

Despite my insistence that you put your own personal style and preferences on hold, you do get to have some FUN making choices once the FOUNDATION of your visual identity is set. Once you have a color family, font, and concept for a logo that supports the rest of your core identity, you are free to make choices based on what YOU think looks good. For example, once we determined that the blue color family was right for SERHANT. (we'll go deeper into this in a minute), I could choose a shade of blue that spoke to me. There are about a billion shades of blue to choose from. I dismissed certain shades for being too Smurfy, too Blue Man Group, and too Tiffanyesque (certain shades of blue are already associated very specifically with certain brands and are familiar to everyone; Tiffany has even trademarked its signature color because it is associated so closely with their brand) before we settled on the classy, fresh, and bold shade of cobalt. Once my design team established that a font from the sans serif family made the most sense, I narrowed down my choices and ultimately selected Montserrat. We settled on the foundation of our logo first—the concept, shape, and meaning. When I was presented with seventy different versions, I taped each one I liked to the wall of my office so that I saw them constantly. Eventually, I was able to narrow it down to the one that looked best to me. Making design decisions is fun, but that fun yields great results only once you've established the right foundation. Okay, are we clear on all that? Great. Now it's your turn to explore the three main elements of visual identity. READY, SET, GO!

CREATING YOUR VISUAL IDENTITY

VISUAL IDENTITY: A FEW BACK STORIES

Mike Evans, cofounder of GrubHub and founder of Fixer, gave his designer some unusual instructions when he was working on GrubHub's visual identity. "I told the designer I wanted GrubHub's visuals 'to look like *South Park* . . . but Smurfier.' The designer looked at me like I had three heads, like what does that mean? I wanted the look to be a more kid-friendly version of *South Park*." Mike goes on to explain that when they were first building the brand, they didn't take themselves too seriously, and the brand was about fun. And while a lot of work ultimately went into creating the visual identity, they were aiming for a quirky and irreverent feel.

Griffin Thall, cofounder and CEO of Pura Vida, designed the brand's very first logo himself, and he wanted the visuals to emphasize the idea that Pura Vida bracelets are one-of-a-kind creations. "I designed the first logo when we came back from Costa Rica. The logo showed a very thin, lightweight, natural font style, and we had that logo for about five years. Then our designer said, 'Why don't we just hand draw the logo over the typeface?' So now if you look at it, it's an imperfect logo. . . . Every bracelet is different and unique, so why should the typeface look super rigid and perfect on every edge? That's why the logo has a natural look."

Lewis Morgan, cofounder of Gymshark and executive chair of AYBL Group, took a direct approach, aiming for a look that was as strong as their workout-loving customers with a little dash of fun. "If you look at Gold's Gym or Pit Bull Gym, it's a big, strong man with muscles or a big tensing dog. We wanted to emulate what was selling, so we made a shark with big biceps that is featured on all of our clothes. It is eye-catching and relevant to our customers, and anytime anyone looked at shirts from any of those other brands, it was almost impossible not to think of *our* brand."

THE THREE ELEMENTS OF VISUAL IDENTITY

1. Color

Color psychology is real, and color is yet another tool to help you connect your brand with your desired audience. Colors have the power to make us all feel things, good and bad, and color does play an important role in how customers or clients perceive your brand. Colors are never just colors, as they have the power to impact our decisions. Understanding the feelings that each color represents can help you choose a color that pulls your desired audience to you. We've all had reactions to colors. Bright green grass and a soft blue sky on a warm spring day are cheering after a long winter. A certain shade of red puts a smile on your face because it reminds you of the bike you had when you were a kid. You can picture your ten-year-old self flying down a hill on that shiny red bike (red is associated with excitement, energy, and action). Many of us can remember the bright orange splotch with *Nickelodeon* written over it in big letters—orange is the color that's associated with creativity, confidence, warmth, and friendliness . . . which are ideal feelings to convey if you want to get kids to watch your shows. While you obviously can't predict how each individual person is going to react to your color scheme (there is nothing you can do if someone has banned the color yellow from their life because an evil ex-boyfriend wore it allllllll the time), you can refer to color psychology when making

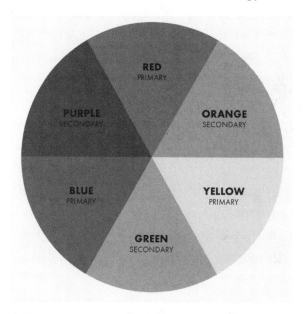

Red	Orange	Yellow	Green	Blue
Excitement	Confidence	Creativity	Nature	Trust
Strength	Success	Happiness	Healing	Peace
Love	Bravery	Warmth	Freshness	Loyalty
Energy	Sociability	Cheer	Quality	Competence

Pink	Purple	Brown	Black	White
Compassion	Royalty	Dependable	Formality	Clean
Sincerity	Luxury	Rugged	Dramatic	Simplicity
Sophistication	Spirituality	Trustworthy	Sophistication	Innocence
Sweet	Ambition	Simple	Security	Honest

choices that are right for your brand. Here is the same color chart I used when choosing cobalt blue for SERHANT.

If you've ever gone to a paint store to buy green paint, you know it's not that simple. Do you want mint green, emerald green, forest green, tea green, olive green, apple green, or one of the other nine hundred versions? Each color listed in the chart above has endless shades and variations that could convey more nuanced emotions and ideas. I chose blue for SERHANT. because it conveys trust, peace, loyalty, and competence. I eventually selected cobalt blue because it felt bold, bright, crisp, solid, and modern—I liked the statement that shade would make when combined with the other qualities that already come along with the blue family. When people see my logo or any of our branded communications, I want them to immediately think *success*, and I also want the feeling of trust to shine through. Ultimately, I want people to feel comfortable putting the sale of their home in my hands, knowing I'm the best person for the job. Once you choose a color family that works well with your adjectives and brand personality, you can refine further until you find a variation that works for you.

2. Typeface

A font isn't just a font—it's yet another way to show off your brand's personality. When I started this process, it was overwhelming. It seems like there is a never-ending pool of fonts to choose from—there are thousands of them! To avoid losing your mind, narrow it down. Start with the four major font families. Just like any human family, the four major font families have their own vibes and personalities. There is serif, sans serif, script, and slab serif. Serif fonts feature tiny projections that finish off each

SERIF		SANS SERIF	
Personality	**Examples**	**Personality**	**Examples**
• Traditional	• Baskerville	• Modern	• Futura
• Sophisticated	• Didot	• Straightforward	• Avenir
• Practical	• Adobe Garamond	• Understanding	• Helvetica
• Important	• Times New Roman	• Universal	• Verdana
SCRIPT		**SLAB SERIF**	
Personality	**Examples**	**Personality**	**Examples**
• Elegant	• *August Script*	• Bold	• Josefin Slab
• Classic	• *Pinyon*	• Contemporary	• Bodoni
• Personal	• *Pt Fasco*	• Trendy	• Courier
• Stylish	• *Snell Roundhand*	• Friendly	• Rockwell

letter and tend to be viewed as more traditional, sophisticated, or even practical (the sentence you just read features serif fonts). Sans serif letters (you guessed it, the ones without the projections) are more modern in feel. **Slab serifs feature thick block-like letters,** *while script fonts are slightly whimsical in feel.* For **SERHANT.** we went with Montserrat, which falls under the sans serif family because of its straightforward, modern, and universal feel. I've included the font personality chart we used when building SERHANT. Look at the different personalities and decide which family is the best match for your brand, then explore all the options that fall under that family.

3. Logos

Want to have your mind blown? The average person encounters somewhere between six thousand and ten thousand ads a day. That is so many ads, and that means we're seeing a crazy number of logos every single day of our lives. The logo you create for your brand has to be visually appealing and communicate your message with one quick glance, all while managing to stand out in this never-ending parade of logos. It's a lot to ask of a symbol, character, design, or, in my case, a big cobalt-blue letter *S*. But when a great logo is matched to a brand's *true purpose*, that combination can create a huge BANG. Think about the Nike swoosh. We all know what it looks like. It's everywhere, and it's simple, clear, and immediately recognizable. But there's more to the power of the Nike logo than the iconic swoosh. That logo represents speed, action, and accomplishment, which is a perfect expression of Nike's brand personality. Nike shoes are practically screaming at you, *If you buy me, you'll be swift! You'll get things DONE with me on your feet.* It all ties together beautifully. However, if you slap a big Nike swoosh on the front door of your cupcake shop, it doesn't automatically become the best-selling cupcake shop in the world (plus, Nike would be mad). It doesn't make any sense—nothing about that swoosh connects to "delicious cupcakes." When a logo is not attached to the core of its brand, it won't have the same potency. A great logo alone isn't enough; it needs to connect back to its core identity to make a real and lasting impact.

GET THE PROCESS GOING

If you're like me, you are not a graphic designer, and it can be hard to know how or where to begin. I knew exactly what my core identity was, but translating that into a physical symbol that communicates my message definitely wasn't something I could do on my own. I worked with my in-house design team as well as an outside designer and learned so much. You do not need an in-house design team to do this. There are amazing resources out there that can design a logo for you—99Designs, Canva, or Fiverr, just to throw out a few names. Here's all my advice about pre-logo planning.

Step one: Get inspired

The very first step is to familiarize yourself with what kind of logos you like and what kind of design speaks to you. If mood boards are your thing, it's a great way to start. Pinterest is also a goldmine of inspiration. Collect all and any logos that spark your interest in one place. Okay, now stop for one second. I know what you're thinking, and before you press SEND on an angry email to me, just listen for a second. I *know* I told you earlier that building a visual identity isn't about your personal likes and feelings. That's why I'm going to ask you to deliberately pay attention to WHAT you like about each logo. If you have the Tesla logo front and center in your mood board, is it because a) you think it looks cool or b) some element of the logo helps convey your brand message? Please tell me you chose B. You did, right? Every logo that catches your eye must be subject to the same question: Will some part of this relate back to my brand's message?

PRO TIP: DON'T GET LOST IN LOGO LAND

While it is important to familiarize yourself with logos that work, you could literally spend the rest of your life searching for visuals that inspire you. Don't let yourself get consumed by this activity or you'll never see the finish line. I recommend giving yourself a reasonable due date to keep this process moving along. Two weeks tops if you're doing this on your own.

Step two: Research designers

When seeking expertise outside of my skill set, I always turn to my own network first. A simple email asking WHO LOVES THEIR GRAPHIC DESIGNER? is sure to yield some results. Local businesses are also a great resource. Take note of any businesses in your town that have fantastic logos, and ask who designed them. I realize that sometimes budgets get in the way, but there are ways around this. Consider reaching out to a local design school through their career services center. You might be able to connect with a talented student who is just getting started and will be more affordable than a seasoned designer. Just remember that whichever route you take, your logo is a long-term investment in your brand. While it is an upfront out-of-pocket cost, you're going to use your logo for years and years!

Once you find a designer, get clear on what you're paying for right off the bat. Some designers work on an hourly rate, while others offer a package rate. You also need to know what you're actually getting in the form of files. You want to have versions that work for the web and for print. You'll also want color and grayscale so that you can print clearly in both color and black and white. I recommend having one design that works well with a light background and one with dark to cover all your bases. Remember, your graphic designer is not a mind reader. Be open about what you want—share information about your core identity and show examples of the other logos that inspired you. It's also important to be clear and upfront. If your designer presents you with a logo featuring a lobster, don't say, *Well, maybe we can tweak this or change the color* if what you really mean is *I appreciate this attempt, but I'd prefer to lose the lobster and replace it with something different. Maybe an octopus. Can we discuss other ideas?* There's nothing worse than having your time wasted—and theirs (especially if they are getting an hourly rate)! Clear and upfront for the win.

PRO TIP: CREATE A STYLE GUIDE TO MAINTAIN VISUAL CONSISTENCY

None of this work you did to create your visual identity matters—the colors, the typeface, the logo itself—if you don't use it ALL THE TIME! Your brand will come off as messy if your font is Times New Roman one day followed by Helvetica the next. To ensure that every single thing you put out into the world is RIGHT, create a style guide and USE IT. A style guide is simply a document where you keep all the guidelines for your visual identity. This way, there will be consistency across the board no matter who is producing content for your brand. The SERHANT. style guide features our logo, specific colors, and typography, and we refer to it constantly.

YOUR EMAIL ADDRESS SAYS A LOT
ABOUT YOUR BRAND

Since this chapter focuses on all the visual impressions your brand makes, we need to take a minute to talk about something very important. We aren't going to talk about websites, since there are about a billion resources that can provide you with great advice about building a website, but it's often while planning a website that one very important aspect of your brand is overlooked. PLEASE PLEASE PLEASE NEVER EVER USE A GMAIL, YAHOO, OR HOTMAIL email address for professional purposes. Sure, go ahead and use hipsterfarmer@gmail.com for buying the supplies you need to tend to your flock of chickens, but do not under any circumstances use such an email address for your free-range egg business. No one—no one!—would take my best and final offer for a multimillion-dollar apartment seriously if my email address was something like badassbroker62@ aol.com. Not having a properly branded email address is a huge red flag that you are NOT TAKING YOUR BRAND SERIOUSLY. And if you don't take your brand seriously, who will? You do take yourself seriously, right?

It is important to own your personal domain and establish an email address associated with that domain name. This goes beyond branding; it's about presenting the most polished, professional version of you at every step of the client-customer interaction. Sure, free email domains are fine for personal correspondence, but using your own domain adds a level of security and professionalism that will help you stand out from the crowd.

Here are some examples using my name.

ryan@ryanserhant.com (this is my main email address)
rs@serhant.com
rserhant@ryanserhant.com

All those email addresses are easily connected to me, and they are very easy to remember and share.

It's important to think about your email signature too. I use a simple format—it's neat, clean, and clear. If it makes sense for your brand to add degrees because they pertain directly to your business (think: physician, psychologist, chiropractor), then do it. Alas, no one needs to see that you graduated magna cum laude with a bachelor's degree in poetry every time you have an email exchange. If you want to add an accolade, go for it, but only if it's especially compelling, like "One of the top orthopedists according to *Orthopedist's Digest*" or "Voted best new clothing boutique in *Clothing Boutique Monthly*." "Best son ever" or "office bowling league champion of '22" isn't going to help you reel in new business.

EMAIL SIGNATURE

Name	**Ryan Serhant**
Title/license held	**Licensed Real Estate Broker**
Company name/logo*	**SERHANT.**
Preferred phone contact*	**o.** (646) 480-7665
Website	**w.** serhant.com
Links to social media accounts	instagram	linkedin	youtube	facebook	twitter

*You may have two lines for this section – one for your office and one for your mobile.

Wow. That was a lot of very specific and technical information, but it is all important! Following this process will add another big layer of professionalism and polish to your brand, and it will yield huge results. As someone who has experienced what happens when you do things haphazardly (nothing) and the correct way (a huge boost in business), I can say with confidence that this work is SO worth it. Now, when I think back on my purple days, I can't help but wish someone had told me that my Vespa-inspired brand wasn't taking me anywhere other than to my next appointment, and by the time I got there I smelled like city bus exhaust. I wanted success so badly, but I didn't understand that I had the power to build a meaningful brand of my own. I didn't need to wait for something big to happen. I didn't need years of experience selling real estate, the help of a huge branding company, or an enormous budget to create a brand. You've done it the right way, and now you can create a visual identity that will snag clients' attention and keep them coming back to your brand again and again. It's time to take that amazing brand that's budding inside of you and unleash it. There is nothing more to wait for; the time is now. Dig in, coax your brand into shape, and watch as your level of success skyrockets beyond your most outrageous dreams.

You've just finished reading about one of my favorite parts of the SERHANT. Brand Strategy System. In this chapter you have accomplished the following:

Learned about the three elements of visual identity ✔
Started collecting inspiration for your logo ✔
Researched designers ✔
Created a style sheet ✔

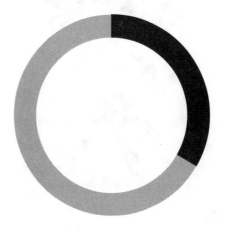

NOW IT'S SYDNEY'S TURN

COLORS

I want Self by Syd to convey feelings like trust, confidence, and competence. I want my clients to feel confident that when they become part of my community, they'll have everything they need to become the best version of themselves.

My selected colors: ORANGE, BLUE, and BROWN.

Thoughts from Sydney

This was the most challenging assessment for me, but very eye-opening. When I initially launched my brand, picking my colors was HARD, and I didn't necessarily set on a single color or set of colors; it was just muted, neutral, yet colorful. I sent so many different combinations of colors for my website to friends and family, and after MANY mixed reviews, I settled on neutral shades I just liked . . . not a ton of thought behind it other than, "I love those colors, they feel like me, and this is *my* brand." Reassessing the colors put the ball back in my customers' court. The colors now are more aligned with the experience and feelings I want my clients to have when they see Self by Syd. And I never thought orange, blue, and brown would be cute . . . but I LOVE the combo I have on my site now.

TYPEFACE

- I want my brand to feel modern and *universal*—like it's accessible to everyone, not intimidating.

- I also love the idea of a secondary style font that's SERIF—the personality of *practical* and *important* also aligns with what I'd like Self by Syd to convey to clients.

My selected font family is SANS SERIF.

Thoughts from Sydney

This was reinforcing for me because I already have sans serif fonts as my primary brand font! I love the way serif fonts look—super classic and elegant—but I also feel that they can be intimidating. The sans serif font felt more approachable, which is an essence of my brand.

CHAPTER 7

A Very Short Chapter That Will Ensure You Never Take a Bad Photograph EVER Again

Headshots and lifestyle photographs (and I didn't forget videos! Videos get a section all to themselves in the next chapter) are a big part of your visual identity, and it's important to get them right. With a few expert tips, you can easily up the quality of your photographs, and you'll never worry about making a weird face or standing so stiffly that you resemble a cardboard cutout ever again.

THE MODERN HEADSHOT

Headshots have never been more important. I used to think of headshots as the glossy 8×10 black-and-white photos that were super expensive and that I brought to every single audition I ever went to. When I first started working in real estate, I assumed my headshot days were behind me (along with my acting career), but I noticed all the brokers who were crazy successful had professional photographs of themselves. Today, a professional headshot is a must for your brand no matter what you do. It's simply another way to make a great first impression, and it gives potential clients and customers a sense of who you are. Headshots can be featured on your website, included in any press you receive, accompany your bio at speaking events, and used on your social media (more on that soon). If you want to give the impression that you set up your career-coaching business yesterday, then by all means, send an awkward, blurry selfie of you with your cat to the local newspaper when you pitch them a story about how impactful coaching can be. The headshot is the face behind the brand (and sometimes it IS the brand), and a bad photograph can negatively impact the rest of your brand identity.

Thankfully, the days of headshots featuring a static pose and ultra-boring background ARE GONE. No more blank-faced photographs in front of dull-as-dishwater backgrounds! Now there is room for some creativity, and you want photographs that give just a hint of your personality without going too far. You certainly don't want to look so stiff and formal that you resemble a mannequin, but you don't want a smile that's so over-the-top ecstatically happy that you are mistaken for the captain of the cheerleading squad. The name of the headshot game is clean, professional, and confident, and I have to tell you that I feel uniquely qualified to give this advice. Being on television and in print media will inspire a person to learn to take a decent picture right quick. There is nothing worse than striking a bad pose, only to know it will be seen by MILLIONS AND MILLIONS of people. In my early days on *Million Dollar Listing New York*, there were times when I'd see myself on camera and stop dead in my tracks. *Wow, that guy is so sad looking. Did someone kidnap his puppy or something? Oh wait, that's me. Shit. Okay, now I have a big smile plastered on my face, but I look sinister, like I'm plotting a takeover of the Empire State Building. Whoa. My posture is terrible! Mom, I'm sorry I didn't listen to you all those times when you told me to sit up straight. I swear I'll never slouch again! Wow. I sit weird. Do I always look that weird when I'm sitting? Now I'm standing weird too. Seriously, is something wrong with me? Do my legs always look so freakishly long? Okay, I look pretty good there. Finally! Now I need to assume that exact same position 24/7 FOR THE REST OF MY LIFE.*

I've had lots of practice when it comes to being filmed and photographed, and after making plenty of bad faces and striking awkward poses I finally learned what works and how to maximize it. While I will soon share my specific secrets about how to pose, getting a great picture starts with being comfortable, and following these simple guidelines will get you into the right mindset:

1. **Your outfit is your secret weapon.** You can use clothes to target the right clients by choosing something that is aligned with both your brand personality and who you are as a professional. Think carefully about your target clients. What kind of outfit will make them feel comfortable and confident connecting with you? For example, if your target client is a high-net-worth banker, be sure to exude your professionalism by wearing something that shows that you effortlessly fit into the world of money and finance. You'd probably want a well-tailored suit in this case. Or, if you are aiming to sell expensive beach properties you can go with a

brightly colored dress or blouse or a collared shirt with the sleeves rolled up. You still need to be professional, but in this case a subtle relaxed vibe works well. A pair of jeans and a T-shirt might be perfect for a dog walker, but not so much for a financial planner. Your outfit is almost like a costume—it adds an additional layer of support to whatever image you are trying to project.

Ask yourself: *Would I hire myself in this outfit?*

2. **Your background must support your vision.** I understand that the best portrait ever taken of you might have been at your wedding, but a beaming picture of you in a wedding gown standing in front of a church isn't going to help you rake in clients for your college essay preparation business. Just like every other single thing we've discussed in this book, your choice of background must support your vision! When my brand vision was to be the most successful agent in New York City, I used a classic New York City cobblestone street as my background. Now that my vision is more global, I've switched to a more neutral background that isn't tied to any specific location. Your choice of location doesn't have to be right on the nose . . . but it needs to *make sense.*

Ask yourself: *Does this background help project my brand personality to the world?*

3. **Find a matching memory.** You're going for professional! Polished! Confident yet approachable! Unless

you are very comfortable being photographed, practice is key, and your smartphone is going to save you lots of time and energy. Ask a friend to help you do a dry run and go crazy taking photographs. What works, what doesn't? When a particular pose is working, note how you feel! Are you relaxed, excited, hopeful, or happy? Think of a memory from your life that puts you in the same emotional mindset and *use it*. Are you smiling perfectly because you're remembering your favorite vacation? Are you channeling the right mix of calm and confident because you are thinking about that time you nailed that pitch at work? Lean on that memory during your photoshoot to exude the right vibe.

Ask yourself: *What event in my life made me feel the way I want to appear in my headshot?*

LIFESTYLE PHOTOGRAPHS

Lifestyle photography has never, ever been more important. Audiences want to see brands in action. That means photographs of you *being your brand*. An example of that could be a photograph of me getting ready for an open house, a chef prepping ingredients for a meal, or a writer sitting in her garden with a book and a glass of rosé. Lifestyle photographs provide your audience with a glimpse of your inner life that shows *what your brand looks like out in the wild*. Lifestyle photography also includes photographs that express the essence of what your brand is . . . stylish living rooms, beautifully set tables, bowls of pasta, cute dogs, cuter babies, an artfully cluttered desktop, gardens, home gyms, air travel, books arranged by color, pool parties, fancy cocktails, and perfectly disheveled early-morning hairdos are just a few examples of the kinds of photographs that we all see in our social media feeds. There are a few reasons why lifestyle photography is essential to building a brand that makes money:

1. Lifestyle photographs show how a product or service can enhance your life. For example, seeing a cozy photo of a person lounging by a crackling fire, wrapped in a blanket, can inspire the thought, *Oh, that chunky knitted weighted blanket is exactly what I need to relax on a cold winter evening. I'm buying that right now!*

2. Lifestyle photographs bring out the human behind the brand. Seeing a photograph of a fitness influencer looking exhausted after a tough workout is a reminder that even fitness influencers face challenges with workouts. These *I'm just like you* moments can promote a stronger connection between a brand and its audience.

3. Lifestyle photographs add variety to your social media feeds. You've got to mix things up to keep your audience engaged. If I shared ONLY photographs of apartments, I'd bore my audience, and I wouldn't be showing all sides of my brand.

WAIT. WILL THIS PHOTOGRAPH RUIN MY LIFE?

It seems like everyone is talking about authenticity today, but what does that really mean when it comes to using photographs while creating and maintaining a personal brand? A deep dive into authenticity is right around the corner in this book, but it definitely comes into play with photographs, so let's discuss it before you do something you regret. The word *authentic* is no longer just for designer handbags and well-prepared, delicious international cuisines. Today, more often than not, the word *authenticity* is used to describe *people*, and how does that extend to photographs? *Beauty influencer A shows us what she looks like first thing in the morning without any makeup on! Fitness influencer B did his entire workout live and then made a protein shake with pulverized diamonds and bananas he grew in the greenhouse he built with his bare hands! I wasn't really a big fan of A-list celebrity so and so, but when he posted that video of himself crying while watching the finale of* Dawson's Creek, *my heart just opened right up! THEY ARE SOOOOOO AUTHENTIC!* But when does authentic go too far, hopping right over the line into TMI or just plain bullshit? As someone who has shown their butt on national television (and lived to regret it), I can tell you that the answer isn't always clear. However, the following guidelines can help you determine if an authentic lifestyle photograph adds the right touch of vulnerability or if you'll regret it forever:

1. Will anyone be embarrassed (including yourself)?
2. The internet is forever. Are you okay with this photograph existing in perpetuity? ARE YOU SURE?
3. Is it a flat-out lie? Thinking of renting a private jet for a selfie? Just don't do it.
4. Does this photograph relate in some way to the core of your brand? For example, is it crucial we see footage of your dental surgery?

5. Are you hitting your audience over the head with something? Photos of your kitten might be a huge hit with your audience, but don't lean on the cuteness so hard that the purpose of your brand gets watered down.

PRACTICE, RELAX, AND JUST GO FOR IT

While these are important guidelines to follow, just remember to relax and have fun. This is a photo shoot, not a root canal. The more you let yourself ease into the process, the better the results you're going to have. You can also lean on your photographer to help you project an image that fits these criteria and also fits in with your brand personality. For specific tips, refer to our handy posing guide below for help! I've also included templates at the end of this chapter to help you stay organized during your photo shoot.

1. Chin down, ears forward! This will help accentuate your facial features to make you appear confident, yet approachable.

2. Angle Your Shoulders Slightly: Work with your photographer to make sure your shoulder isn't too angled or too straight – a slight angle is most flattering.

The quarter turn is an easy, natural look

3. Arm Placement: Don't just let them hang there—you'll look stiff and uncomfortable. Crossing your arms or putting a hand on your hip or in your pocket will look more natural and confident.

If in doubt, cross your arms

4. Smile! Practice in the mirror—experiment with a more open or closed mouth, and with the broadness of your smile.

Ryan doesn't look as friendly with a closed mouth

5. Most importantly, relax. As Ryan always says, people hate being sold but love shopping with friends. A relaxed, friendly headshot will help humanize you—but be sure to stay true to your brand personality.

Lean in slightly to appear less stiff

6. Putting it all together!

1. For seated shots, experiment with different angles, arm placement, and leg placement. It is okay to look like you are relaxed, or having fun—however, avoid looking sloppy or too informal. Remember, these are still an important marketing tool!

Talia is hunched over and closed off

2. Practice different angles: Avoid staring at the camera straight on or standing/sitting too far back from the camera—this often comes off as cold or unfriendly.

Sitting or standing against a wall appears as though you are backing away

3. Like with your headshot, relax! Practice in the mirror to find poses that let you shine. Show some personality, have a little fun, and stay true to your brand personality.

Be mindful of slouching

4. Most importantly, make your photographer a collaborator in this project to make sure you are happy with the final product. Build a working relationship with a photographer you trust: it will serve you well over time.

A VERY SHORT CHAPTER ON PHOTOGRAPHS

Use the following checklist to ensure you've planned the most important aspects of your lifestyle photoshoot.

Photographer Selected and Confirmed

☐ Name: _____

☐ Contact Info: _____

_____

Hair/Makeup Artist Selected and Confirmed

☐ Name: _____

☐ Contact Info: _____

_____

Location(s) Selected and Confirmed

☐ Location 1 Address: _____

_____

☐ Contact Info (if needed): _____

_____

☐ Location 2 Address: _____

_____

☐ Contact Info (if needed): _____

_____

Wardrobe Stylist Selected and Confirmed

☐ Name: _____

☐ Contact Info: _____

_____

Date of Photoshoot:

_____

Start time:

_____

End time:

_____

Weather forecast: *(helpful for determining lighting/styling needs)*

_____

Specific Wardrobe Pieces to Bring:

☐ Shirts/Blouses

☐ Jackets

☐ Pants

☐ Dresses/Skirts

☐ Shoes

☐ Accessories

BRAND IT LIKE SERHANT

LOCATION	WARDROBE	CONCEPT
1.	1.	1.
2.	2.	2.
3.	3.	3.
4.	4.	4.
5.	5.	5.
6.	6.	6.
7.	7.	7.
8.	8.	8.
9.	9.	9.
10.	10.	10.
11.	11.	11.
12.	12.	12.

Congratulations on making it to the end of Phase One! You wrapped up this phase by accomplishing the following:

Planning an outfit ✔

Considering backgrounds for headshots and lifestyle photos ✔

Thinking of a memory that always makes you smile ✔

Practicing for your photo shoot ✔

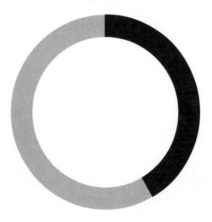

NOW IT'S SYDNEY'S TURN

PHOTOGRAPHY

My photo style has definitely evolved along with my brand, and initially I modeled it after photoshoots I'd seen from my friends in the industry. What I feel I'm missing and will be adding are more high-quality lifestyle shoots. My focus to this point has been headshots, or photos of me with blank space to layer things like promotional messaging, or with room for website elements to lay over them if I were to use it as a banner image on my site.

Now, I want to add quality photos that depict the versatility of my brand—photos that help tell the story of my AND, my process, and the value I can provide. Not just me! This could look like:

1. Photos of me working with clients
2. Photos of me teaching a group class
3. Photos of me prepping my meals in the kitchen
4. Photos of me exploring NYC
5. Photos of me working from a café or at the office
6. Photos of me mid-workout

I'm reapproaching my photoshoot needs from the perspective of the characters I have now: The Coach, The Busy Professional, and The Athlete.

PHASE TWO:

Consistency Is the Key

CHAPTER 8

The Five Families: Facebook, Instagram, LinkedIn, YouTube, and TikTok

Consistency is like the oil that keeps your brand moving along like a finely tuned sports car. Imagine the kind of car that glides along smoothly with a gentle purr from the engine—but also has the power to hit eighty miles per hour in just a few seconds. Smooth, steady, and powerful. Consistency is what supports a brand as it moves forward, and it's also what can propel it to fantastic new heights. When it comes to social media, it is also what makes the difference between having a few customers follow you, maybe occasionally liking one of your posts, and building a thriving audience that draws in business, creates awareness for your brand, and helps you earn more money. Before we get into a discussion about how to use consistent content to increase your brand's awareness, I'm going to touch on each of the platforms I use and share the most important wisdom I've gleaned about them as I've used social media to build SERHANT.

NO MORE EXCUSES

Social media's effectiveness as a marketing tool is simply not up for discussion. It works . . . and it is yet another example of one of my all-time favorite phrases: *When you take care of the work, the work takes care of you.* In this case, the work you put in by posting regular content takes care *of you* by increasing your visibility and bringing you new business. So, whether or not you enjoy looking at beautiful Instagram photographs of other people's dogs/babies/gardens/artful cappuccinos/homemade sourdough bread/beach vacations (the list goes on forever), you need to embrace this revenue-building and lead-generating opportunity NOW. If the mere thought of posting a photograph from your trek up Machu Picchu makes you want to throw up, think of it this way—there are approximately 3.8 billion people using social media. THAT IS ALMOST HALF THE POPULATION OF EARTH. Also, advertisers spend nearly $42 billion a year to feed consumers targeted ads, again because there's the potential to reach HALF THE PLANET.

If that isn't enough to convince you, maybe this will. If you work your social media accounts consistently and effectively, it's possible you can kick some (or all) of those dusty old lackluster lead-generation tactics to the curb. Drawing more business from social media can mean less time cold-calling strangers. (I can't possibly be the only person who would rather shave off my eyebrows than do that, right?) It is also within the realm of possibility that you can open a revenue stream by simply posting and optimizing social media content on a daily basis. MONEY JUST FOR POSTING! So, is it really that much of a hardship to post a photograph of you in your climbing gear as an entry into this world that can ultimately make your life much easier and bring you more money?

NO ONE CAN KEEP UP WITH SOCIAL MEDIA

In New York City Mafia lore of the early twentieth century, there were five families, each with its own specific territory and organizational structure. These five families would engage in power struggles both internal and external and would often fight over territories. If you were a member of one of the five families, you needed a few specific traits to survive: you needed to be loyal (everything they were doing was illegal, so they kept their mouths shut), possess good networking skills (to forge relationships with police, labor unions, other mobsters, etc.), have solid business acumen (those pounds of cocaine won't sell themselves), and have the discipline to manage all those things without being garroted with piano wire. *No thank you.* As soon as one power dispute ended (possibly with gunfire), the status quo of the five families would be completely changed, and the Goodfellas would have to figure everything out ALL OVER AGAIN.

Thankfully, struggling to navigate the five families of social media is unlikely to result in a hit—but it can feel like you're in a never-ending pattern of shifting power dynamics. *Wait a minute, Twitter isn't number one anymore? So, Instagram has taken control? What about Facebook? Oh, they're still in the game but might have lost some of their territory because the kids prefer TikTok. Got it. Hold on, though. . . . Is it true that TikTok might be banned? What family will fill those shoes? Do you know who they are so I can get in on that action early? By the way, what ever happened to MySpace?*

Navigating the five most popular social media platforms will require you to stay on your toes. Honestly, sometimes I really wish I had a time machine. By the time this book is printed, I could be totally embarrassed that I didn't know about Hoppity-Hop, Chatter Chat, and SoothSlayer (I made those up, but it is absolutely within the realm of possibility that this chapter will soon belong in a time capsule). Social media changes quickly. I mean, even as I'm writing this, Meta just launched Threads, a competitor to Twitter, and then Twitter decided to rebrand to x.com?!* Plus, we have no idea what platforms will exist in the near future. Who knows? Maybe we'll all be able to shoot holograms of ourselves into people's living rooms with the click of a button. (Wait. We can't do that yet, can we?) This is worth repeating. We all need to keep in mind that while social media is an amazing marketing tool, it requires flexibility and being open to change. Don't be afraid to explore, experiment, and see what works best for you because the second you think you know exactly what you're doing, SURPRISE! Everything changes. AGAIN.

The good news is that the tactics we are talking about in this chapter can likely be adapted and applied to any exciting new platforms that come our way . . . including holograms. If you're thinking, *Well, if this is all going to change, what is the point?! I mean, why bother?!* the answer is, because these platforms are incredibly powerful tools that everyone has access to. Finding success and an audience here is only going to make your life

---

* The change from Twitter to X happened in the middle of writing this book. I mean, WOW. What a way to destroy a brand!

easier as new options pop up. And all of us (barring anyone who has the ability to time travel) are in the same boat! So, please just keep all this in mind as I outline current best practices for operating within the five families.

THE FIVE FAMILIES: A QUICK AND EASY PRIMER

Consider this a simple introduction to the most common social media platforms being used right now. Then we can get on with the important work of bringing your personal brand to life. Following are no-nonsense descriptions of each of the five families, and I've shared why I like to use them.

Instagram: Arguably the best social platform for quickly sharing your life with your fans/audience in bite-size pieces (photos, short-form videos, stories, etc.). This is the platform where my biggest audience lives. Whenever I'm thinking about new posts, Instagram is at the top of my mind.

Facebook: All of the above, BUT with a slightly older demographic (40+).

YouTube: The single greatest platform for creating long-form video content, and one of the only platforms where content has true longevity (you could upload a video of your masterful technique for folding fitted sheets, and it could still get views three years from now). This is a key platform for my real estate property tours, and now for my long-form talking head videos where I like to dig deep about all things business. It's also a place to park videos of my podcast.

TikTok: Arguably the single best (and easiest!) platform for quick growth (at least for now). If you've ever met anyone currently in high school, you are likely aware that this is very popular among people in their teens. It also has many fans who are in their thirties, which is a crucial target audience for massive brands. This platform has helped make my brand more monetizable because it brings in brand deals.

LinkedIn: Think of this as Instagram/Facebook for business. In many ways it's like a slightly longer-form version of Twitter that puts more emphasis on images, videos, and carousels. This is where I establish myself as more than a real estate broker. I like to share what I've learned about business and technology, and it's a great place to build relationships with other entrepreneurs and execs (and bonus! These people tend to be high-net-worth individuals looking for fancy homes).

Twitter (Wait. I mean x.com): Okay, I said there were five families (a sixth didn't fit in with my analogy), and if this chapter is destined to be obsolete, can I at least have some fun while it's still relevant? I'd be remiss if I didn't share how I've been using TwitterX. (That's what I'm calling it for now. By the time this book comes out the name could change to #(U$)@ or X-itter, who knows?) I've recently found that TwitterX is a good vehicle for a newsletter-style sort of exchange. Let me explain. I'm not talking about a traditional newsletter (too many characters for TwitterX!), but I can post back-to-back tweets on a single topic or idea, which results in multiple threads . . . and the end result has a newsletter-style feel. It's great for engagement that way. TwitterX is also just good for quick, conversational micro-interactions with people. It's one of the best places for updates, news, and things that are happening NOW. This is not really the place, however, for evergreen content—think quick fleeting thoughts, updates, trends, and news!

Threads: Look, I HAD to at least mention Meta's new app, Threads. To be fair, this literally didn't exist when I came up with this analogy. In short, it's the same thing as TwitterX, but you're interacting with (almost) an entirely different audience. Whereas TwitterX attracts people primarily interested in politics, news, business, and tech, Threads is a version of TwitterX where you can reach the same audience you have on Instagram and Facebook—the ones interested in cat videos, beautiful homes, and that amazing chocolate chip cookie recipe your grandma gave you. So, when I say that my posts on TwitterX and my posts on Threads receive entirely different feedback despite more or less being the same content, it's because I'm speaking to different crowds.

HOW DO THESE PLATFORMS WORK?

Alright, so now that we have a good sense of the platforms we're dealing with, we need to address an important question: How do each of these platforms work? In other words, how can you use each of these to grow an audience and see real results from your content? And this is probably where you hear social media gurus talk about "the algorithm." If each social media platform were one of the five Mafia families, "the algorithm" would be "the Commission." The Commission was a governing group created in 1931 to create consensus and a sense of order among the Mafia families after some particularly bloody infighting and power struggles.

In social media, the algorithm is similar to the Commission in that it is a set of rules that establishes how data behaves. These "rules" are meant to keep things in order and decide how search rankings work and what kinds of advertisements show up. Technically, each social media platform has its own algorithm, but the truth is, they behave so similarly that there's no real point in focusing on the differences. So, let's start with the basics: What is an algorithm? Well, the dictionary definition is "a set of rules to be followed in calculations or other problem-solving operations, especially by a computer." Okay, great . . . but that doesn't exactly shed any sort of illuminating light on what that means for using social media to build our brands, does it? So, here is my unofficial definition of a social media algorithm:

> **The set of rules that are used to determine whether or not your content and profile receive *distribution*, and to *whom* they are distributed.**

Now, it might not surprise you to learn that like everything else in this world, social media algorithms have also gone through some significant transformations over the past decade. For example, think about the early days of TwitterX, Facebook, and Instagram. We're talking wayyyyyyyyy back in 2004 to 2016. Whenever you posted something, it went to the top of everyone's feed so long as they were following you. Algorithms were extremely basic, and content was shown chronologically. Then, in 2011, a little yellow app with a ghost for a logo came onto the scene and added a new layer of complexity. Snapchat made it so that while content was still shown chronologically, it was now time sensitive. They took this to the next level with the launch of Snapchat Stories in 2013, which was the first version of public-facing ephemeral content. Prior to Snapchat Stories, it didn't really matter if you didn't check your socials for a few days because everything that was posted was still going to be there tomorrow, but not anymore. After twenty-four hours, if you didn't see someone's post about *how to fold a fitted sheet in less than fifteen seconds with a broken arm while blindfolded*, it was gone forever. So, as you could guess, Snapchat's user engagement skyrocketed. People were getting real FOMO. No wonder Instagram was so quick to steal the idea.

But then, just a few years later, in 2016, someone at Instagram had an idea that fundamentally changed how we talk about social media platforms and "the algorithm." But before I talk about what that idea was, we need to ask an important question: Why do social media platforms have algorithms to begin with? I mean, why did the Mafia create the Commission? Those may seem completely unrelated, but believe it or not, the answer is the same. And to answer this, we should think about an even simpler question: What's the goal of these social media platforms? Or, to continue with our crime family analogy, what's the goal of the Mafia families? To make money!

While we may not always realize it while looking for new salad recipes on Instagram, ultimately, social media platforms are just for-profit companies. Their goal is to make money and get big returns for their investors. While this may sound like a stupid, obvious digression, this will help completely reframe how you view your social media and content moving forward. So, knowing that these social media companies are in it to make money, why would they invest millions and millions of dollars into developing algorithms? Well, in short, because it helps them make even more money! Almost all these platforms make the vast majority of their revenue through selling ads. Every time you're on social

169

media and you see an ad from Coca-Cola, Ralph Lauren, or even a small mom-and-pop bakery in your neighborhood, that social media platform is making money. But here's the thing: they're able to sell that advertising space only because people like you and me (and everyone else with a cell phone and internet connection!) are using their apps, giving those companies a reason to want to advertise there. THIS is why people say we live in an "attention economy." Your attention is literally being monetized left, right, and center. Anywhere you're "paying attention" online is almost certainly being monetized in one way or another—whether that's being done with ads placed on the platform, brand deals done with influencers, or exclusive content offered through paid subscriptions, your attention is being monetized.

ENTER ENGAGEMENT

So, how does all this play into that Instagram employee's genius idea in 2016? Well, they realized that the best way to get people to stay on their platform—you know, so that they can continue to display ads and make money—is by showing people better, *more engaging* content. If you think about it, chronological content is pretty uninspired. It's relevant only because it's new, but there's no more merit to it beyond its newness. In 2015, if I decided to tweet ten thousand times a day, I probably would've been the only person you saw in your TwitterX feed (until you decided to unfollow me for being annoying). So, in late 2016, Instagram changed its algorithm to display content based on the amount of engagement it received in the form of likes, comments, and shares. All of a sudden, when you went onto the app, you weren't seeing your aunt's photos of her pet guinea pig (or at least not as often); instead, you were seeing all the photos and videos that other people were engaging with. This created a kind of "content meritocracy." From cute cat videos to inspirational rants from your favorite motivational speaker, your social media feed had changed almost in its entirety. The content that received the most engagement would also receive the most distribution from the algorithm. And it's for this reason that people started to follow "influencers" and "content creators." Prior to late 2016, these terms were seldom used, and now we see them everywhere! Think about it: in the early days of social media, you probably followed only your friends, family, coworkers, and colleagues, and maybe a small handful of brands you really liked. Compare that with today, where you may not even know the majority of the people you follow. Needless to say, this algorithm shift was a HUGE success for Instagram because people started to spend more and more time on the platform. So, naturally, every other social media platform followed suit, implementing new engagement-based algorithms. Got it?

At this point, social media usage was at its peak. Every time you opened one of those apps, you were immediately met with the most engaging content from the people you followed, and anytime you weren't using the platforms, you had FOMO because you risked missing the ephemeral content people were posting to their stories. And, of course, with the increase in social media usage came an increase in advertising dollars for all the big social media companies. They have us hooked . . . almost. There is one problem with an engagement-based algorithm: it isn't addicting enough. If you sign up for Instagram and follow a bunch of friends, family, and random content creators, your feed will be only as interesting as the people you follow. Sure, Instagram (like all the other social media platforms) will automatically show you the top-performing content from those people, but what if they all kind of suck? Or, what if their content is decent, but there are other people on the platform making similar-style content that is miles better? You'd never know! As a result, even with an engagement-based algorithm, it's pretty easy to get bored and stop using the app. And that's where the final evolution of the algorithm comes in.

THE EVOLUTION OF THE ALGORITHM

TikTok took the world by storm. It might have started as a low rumble of thunder that we thought would pass over, but some of us who were reluctant to download the app in 2018–2019 because "it's for kids" and "it's just a bunch of dancing" were very wrong. Now, practically everyone has TikTok on their phone. It may not attract the older crowd in the same way Facebook does, for example, but if you're under the age of forty, there's a good chance that you've at least downloaded it at some point. But why is that? How did this app seemingly come out of nowhere and become a sensation all around the world? Frankly, I could write a chapter on this alone, but for the sake of staying on topic, here's the short answer: the TikTok algorithm was better than anything we had seen before. TikTok took things a step further than Instagram's engagement-based algorithm; they decided, "You know what? These people don't even know what they like, and with the amount of data that we have on our users, WE know what they like *better* than they do." So,

TikTok took a different approach. Their algorithm was still engagement-based, but instead of focusing just on likes, comments, and shares, they decided to focus on "watch time" as the most important metric. However, rather than having the home page/feed showcase the most-engaged content from the people you follow, they decided they were going to show you the most-engaged content from *anyone* that they thought you may be interested in. Every time you like, comment, share, and even watch a video on TikTok, the algorithm tries to show you more content like it. And thus the "For You" page was born—a feed curated specifically *for you*, based not on the people you follow but on the content you interact with the most. Lo and behold, when TikTok blew up in popularity while we were all locked indoors during the pandemic, every other social platform saw this as an opportunity to make the same algorithmic changes. So now, when you go on Facebook, Instagram, TwitterX, TikTok, or YouTube, most of the content you see isn't even from people you follow—it's from people that each social media platform *thinks* you might enjoy.

PRO TIP: DO NOT PAY FOR FOLLOWERS

If my explanation of algorithms wasn't enough to convince you that having THE MOST followers isn't the main goal, keep in mind that if you buy followers, you will be getting random people who do not necessarily fit in with your desired audience, and you risk alienating your real audience if they find out you bought followers.

The evolution of the algorithm has massive implications for content creation and what YOU can do to build your brand. For starters, the algorithm no longer prioritizes followers. This is why you can come across creators with hundreds of thousands or even millions of *real* followers (not the bots that some people pay for—again, bad idea!), and they'll post a video that gets only a few thousand views. This even happens to me from time to time. Sometimes I'll post a video to TikTok or YouTube #shorts (YouTube's in-app TikTok competitor) only for it to get ten thousand views—meanwhile, keep in mind that I have millions of followers. But the algorithm has made it clear: "I don't care about how many followers you have. I care about how good your content is." And the beauty in this is that it means that *everyone* has a shot. I really mean this when I say it: even if you're starting out with creating content *today*, you could beat me or any other big-time creator in your industry. I mean, one of my longtime employees, Adrian Vasquez, who has been my creative director for the past five years, gained over 1.5 million followers across his social media in less than eight months, and he was basically starting from zero!

So, how did Adrian do it? He just started creating interesting, fun, and engaging content. And when TikTok, Instagram, and YouTube saw that tons of people were watching the full length of his videos, leaving likes and comments, and even sharing the videos with friends, the algorithm decided to show them to even more people. And it kept growing.

Everyone has a chance to make it big on social media. If you have a phone with a decent camera and microphone, you too can win big on social. You just need to start creating consistent content (the word *consistent* is KEY), and I'm going to share my secrets for creating good content next. But more than anything I want you to understand this: THERE ARE NO EXCUSES ANYMORE. There is not a single good reason for not being present on social media. There is no reason that you can't post content right now. That's all you need to do to get started! Then do it again tomorrow, and the next day, and do you know what will happen? Your business will increase and your audience will grow. There's only one *tiny, little* downside . . . you'll wonder why you didn't do this SOONER! Do you want to feel regretful about missed opportunities because you weren't maximizing your social media? I didn't think so, so make today THE DAY.

Congratulations on making it through my crash course in social media platforms! While I expect all this to change, I fully believe that the information I presented will help you navigate JayBird, BadaVoom, GiggleFizz, or whatever platforms the future has in store for us.

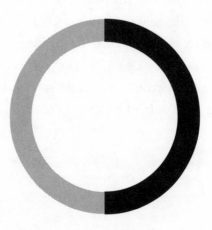

NOW IT'S SYDNEY'S TURN

I spent my early content-creating days for Self by Syd focusing on what type of content was going viral—I was basically trying to beat the algorithm.

But today, instead of trying to beat the algorithm, I embrace it! Because algorithms across social platforms have become so sophisticated, I know I've shared something of value to my target audience if engagement picks up, and then I take the success of that specific piece of content and try to replicate it. If I share something that underperforms, I know I either didn't categorize it correctly or didn't caption it correctly, or it wasn't content that resonated with my audience.

CHAPTER 9

Consistent Content, Your New Best Friend

It was a dark and stormy night. The kind of weather guaranteed to slow down your DoorDash delivery and make getting a taxi impossible. Most of Gotham was tucked in for the night, but Detective Bryan Sellhant was hot on the case, doing surveillance from the warmth of his black SUV. A thief had been slipping into chefs kitchens at open houses all over Manhattan and stealing ice cream from custom-made Sub-Zeros. Could his hunch be right? He lifted his binoculars just in time to see a disgruntled broker walking down the street, boldly carrying a pint of cookies and cream that had recently gone missing from an Upper East Side penthouse. . . .

STOP.

What the actual F?!

If that's what you're thinking, you are having a totally reasonable reaction to a book on branding morphing into a real estate–themed noir-mystery novel (and a really bad one at that). I admit my example is ridiculous, but the fact is we are all wired to expect some level of consistency, and when confronted with a concept, idea, or comment that is 100 percent OUT OF THE BLUE it is jarring, confusing, and maybe even off-putting. Consistency is crucial when building a brand; it promotes credibility and trust, helps the consumer know what to expect (i.e., that your brand is reliable and can be counted on to deliver quality goods and services again and again), and helps cement a positive reputation that promotes connection and referrals. I LOVE REFERRALS! And finally, if you're not consistent about how often you post, ANYONE can pop up and capture the attention of the audience YOU want. While consistency is important across the board, you can start implanting everything that's amazing about your personal brand by focusing on consistent content first. Consistent content is the number one way to get your brand out in front of leads and potential clients.

At SERHANT., **consistent content means regularly scheduled posts featuring brand messaging that's consistent across all platforms.** To put this very plainly, when it comes to posting content for your personal brand, CONSISTENCY IS YOUR BEST FRIEND (sorry BFFs from childhood and college). If you're thinking, *Ryan. Jessica from college will always be my bestie so of course I want her in my social media posts. What's wrong with you?*, please just let me show you how you can get sooooooo much closer to realizing your brand vision when you streamline your social media efforts for maximum impact, and that means consistent brand messaging (which isn't likely to include your college buddies). While trying to reach your brand vision, social media is the tool that will help you accomplish three key things: establish yourself as an *authority* in your industry, remind people constantly that *you're right here*, and provide continual *evidence* that YOU are the go-to human for all things in your industry.

ENGAGEMENT FIRST, FOLLOWERS SECOND

As you're getting started or as you begin to expand on what you're already doing with your social media efforts, we're going to focus on engagement over the size of your audience. Obviously, having an enormous following is beneficial, but like you learned in the previous chapter, you will start to build your audience naturally if you aim for engagement first. Engagement matters—it serves as an indication that you're providing helpful information, fostering relationships, and ultimately shining a spotlight on how everyone needs your personal brand in their lives.

For those of you who are already using social media—whether that means you post the occasional picture of your kids on Facebook or you can be found on TikTok showing off your insanely impressive ability to juggle bowling balls and knives—can we all agree that getting lots of positive feedback in the form of comments and likes feels really good? I am by no means suggesting that any of us should derive a sense of self-worth from Instagram, but I do think that little spark of joy we occasionally feel stems from something that's important for all our personal brands—establishing a positive, engaging, back-and-forth relationship with your audience. Ideally, your audience isn't passively flipping through their feed, scrolling right past your engaging post about spring gardening while sitting in the car, waiting for their kid to get out of school. The goal is to capture attention and get followers to sit up and think, *Oh my God, it never occurred to me that I could take the bottom of my romaine lettuce and use it to grow another romaine lettuce! I'm going to be so healthy thanks to this miraculous, never-ending supply of free salad ingredients that I grow myself. This Instagram gardener is a genius, and I am going to tell her I think so right now by leaving an appreciative comment. (I'm also sending this video to my mom, sister, brother, BFF, and ultra-health-conscious neighbors.)* This kind of engagement is important for a few reasons. When your audience actively engages with your content, they're connected to your brand message. You are laying the groundwork for a community. And you're increasing reach, because great content gets spread to others (this is the only time you actually want something to be as fast and powerful as a virus).

PEOPLE CONNECT WITH BRANDS, NOT COMPANIES

I am luxury real estate AND media, but if you look at my Instagram feed right now, you're not going to see *only* photographs and videos of fancy apartments and townhouses (but there are certainly some, so call me if you see anything you like!). You might see a clip from a speech where I discussed a topic I want to share with my audience, like fear of failure or how to future-proof your work. There's the goofy compilation video of me and Yuriy (my trusty driver who I could not live without) that

I posted to celebrate our tenth anniversary of working together. You'll see pictures from my vacations with Emilia, me with Zena and about nine million balloons at her fourth birthday party (I got carried away when I placed the balloon order), my family in matching Christmas pajamas, and a video of me attempting to body surf down a sand dune in the Middle East. I share personal stories and experiences not because I want to show off my sand surfing skills (which are not good; it's harder than you think) but to open myself up so people have something to engage with and connect to, because people connect with personal brands, not companies. No one would engage with me if the humanness of my brand didn't exist. I mean, who wants to leave a comment on the Instagram feed of a faceless corporate entity? Personal brands are another vehicle to demonstrate your humanity and evoke feelings, and this is something a corporation just can't do.

Griffin Thall, the cofounder and CEO of Pura Vida, who uses the motto "Live free," believes "the DNA of the founder is very similar to the DNA of the business." His social media feeds are a testament to his passion for what his brand represents—living freely and enjoying all the pleasures life has to offer while helping others at the same time. Sure, he has posts about things like the Pura Vida flagship store, and you'll see a rainbow of bracelets on his feed, but he also shares envy-inducing photographs from his own life. Thall enjoys photography and posts photographs he's taken of sandy white beaches, palm trees, and MASSIVE waves that make for killer surfing.

"I think my personal brand has heavily influenced the direction of Pura Vida. The brand started with a carefree, no-goal-in-mind surf trip to Costa Rica after graduating from San Diego State. All we wanted to do was surf, have a couple of beers, explore, get lost, be with our best friends, and just try to live free as much as we can. We had so much fun on that trip." That fun trip inspired an insanely successful business venture. After buying bracelets from an artisan in Costa Rica, Thall and his friends learned that this man and his family were struggling to survive. Wanting to help, the group asked him if he could make four hundred bracelets, which they paid for and brought back to California to sell. "We managed to bring back that fun while helping artisans. We sold bracelets to people, they became trendy on social media, and eventually we got them sold in over five thousand retailers." Thall makes it clear their product isn't just a bracelet—it's a physical symbol that serves as a reminder to live your life with passion. That core value of "live free" is exuded in all of Thall's social media posts. The surfing, snowboarding, and traveling are what inspire the Pura Vida audience to engage with the brand, forging a strong and lasting connection.

EMBRACE THE LEARNING CURVE LIKE
EVERYONE ELSE

In this chapter, you are essentially going to learn how to be the CEO of your own media company. I know that sounds over-whelming. Remember that you are not alone, and there are ways to conquer this feeling! Chef Carla Lalli Music shares that she didn't know what a big undertaking she was in for when she started her personal brand. "I didn't really think about the fact that I was CFO, CEO, head of content and talent, food stylist, and executive producer. I had been doing food videos for a while and I thought, *I know how to do this.* But there was no playbook for what percentage of your Instagram audience is going to become your subscriber base, and from there what percentage of that are you supposed to spend on production and postproduction? I made so many mistakes that first year. But putting myself at the bottom of the learning curve over and over again has been a really important part of my growth."

Truthfully, whether you've been using social media for most of your life or you're just starting now, WE ALL END UP AT THE BOTTOM OF THE LEARNING CURVE. Social media is an ever-changing world, so while your average teenager might be more comfortable figuring out a new platform than your seventy-year-old father, the truth is EVERYONE has to take a step back to figure out something new. There is always a new point of entry when it comes to social media; there is always something new for ALL OF US to figure out. . . . So just take a running leap and hop on the train with the rest of us.

PRO TIP: BE A CONSCIOUS CONSUMER

If you are new to social media or want to use a new plat-form for the first time, the best thing you can do is become a conscious consumer. Analyze what you watch and who you watch, and ask yourself, *WHY?* What's the difference between something you scroll right past versus something that gets your attention? Spending some time just exploring social media is an excellent way to get a sense of how the platforms work and to spark ideas about how you can use them to share your brand.

LET ME SAVE YOUR SANITY

Undeniably, launching a personal brand on social media is a ton of work, but there is a huge advantage to being in the trenches (ideally temporarily!) and learning about all aspects of the process. When chef Alison Roman reflects on the beginning of her personal brand, she recognizes that putting in ALL the work would have made things easier in the long run: "I would have learned to build my website on my own. I would have learned some technical skills that would make things easier for me without having to hire external people (although that can be great too!). I think even if you're not doing it yourself, knowing how to do it makes it easier to communicate what you want when you do hire someone. So, in terms of graphic design, or directing or editing a video, having any firsthand knowledge will make you a more effective communicator, a better boss, a better leader, and you'll know what you're talking about when you're trying to redesign, fix, or change something."

Gary Vaynerchuk, CEO of VaynerMedia, whose social media platforms succeed on a level we all dream of (we'll discuss what success really looks like for social media soon), also recognizes there is value in being directly involved with your content: "I was such an early YouTube star, like so early! I wasn't getting crazy numbers, but solid numbers and even to this day I don't do YouTube well compared to everything else. I don't spend enough time on thumbnails or titles, and it's the only place where I would say I'm not as good of a technician as I am everywhere else because I'm not the one doing it; I'm detached from it. I still write the copy for my own posts, though. And I think a lot of people who are trying to build their brand are trying to have someone else build it for them, and they're detached from it."

I know starting a personal brand means having a just-loaded-up-at-the-all-you-can-eat-buffet level of fullness on your plate, but it's temporary. Think of social media as a new knowledge base that's going to help you bring your personal brand to the next level. And if you have already established a social media presence, ask yourself what else you can learn. What can you do better? Remind yourself that tackling this hurdle of a learning curve is only going to make your life easier in the end. If you feel overwhelmed right now, please don't freak out. Yes, it feels like I'm expecting a lot of you, but when handled in bite-size pieces and on a doable schedule, being the CEO of your own content company becomes manageable. With some practice, creating and posting your content will become a regular (and hopefully fun) part of your routine. This is the same process we use at SERHANT., and have I mentioned we are the most followed real estate brand in the world? (I probably did, but just in case.) Okay, let me break it down for you.

THE CONTENT MATRIX

At SERHANT. we carefully create, plan, and schedule content for our social media accounts because if we want to make an impact and capture the attention of our audience, we need to pop up in their social media feeds on a very regular basis. To keep our content fresh, fun, and interesting but on brand, we use a

Content Matrix—a simple grid that details two crucial things: what our posts have to offer our audience, and the three different sides of me we want to share, which we refer to as "characters."

Ryan's Content Matrix

	Real estate	Entrepreneur and tech CEO	Luxury lifestyle and family man
Entertain	Property tours, property Zoom walkthroughs, deal stories, crazy listing features, archival content	Day-in-the-life, business of influence, social media trends, VLOGS	Luxury features (cars, watches, fashion), celebrity features, social media trends
Educate	Market updates, VLOGS	Start-up stories, conference convos, time hacks/ routines, candid fan moments, VLOGS	Work/life balance flow, workouts, nutrition
Encourage	Transformative work moments, work stories, success stories	Motivational mindset tips, VLOGS	Family moments, Dadurday plans, dad jokes

The purpose of our posts (other than connecting with our audience and community so we can earn more money) is to entertain, educate, and encourage. The "characters" who provide that entertainment, education, and encouragement for our audience are real estate Ryan, entrepreneur/tech CEO Ryan, and luxury lifestyle/family man Ryan. All our content relates back to this matrix—work stories, success stories, time hacks, day-in-the-life moments, posts about luxury goods, dad jokes, and "Dadurday" plans, to name a few. The extra bonus of the Content Matrix is that it contains your thought process. The matrix is literally a black-and-white visual that gives you three areas to play with.

NOW IT'S YOUR TURN

Exercise: Design Your Content Matrix

STEP ONE: *Visualize your target customer and analyze the different ways they see you.*

If you are a florist, it could break down like this:

Character one: Florist

For example, if you are a florist your customers will primarily see you as their go-to person when they need flowers for an event, a friend, special occasions, and when they just want something pretty for the dining room table.

Character two: Design Influencer

Because you have been carefully building your brand, every aspect of your website and store is beautiful and inspires creativity. Customers see you as more than a florist—they see you as someone with a great sense of design that they'd like to emulate.

Character three: Mom

Because you and your store are a presence in your community, your customers also see you as another local mom. In addition to running a thriving business, you are just like the other moms—running off to soccer games, racing to make school pickup, and scheduling play dates.

STEP TWO: Explore what each character can offer your social media audience.

The florist can offer pictures of stunning floral arrangements with background information on how it was put together, tips on how to make flowers live longer, and information about seasonal flowers, such as why everyone should be filling their houses with peonies right now.

The florist can offer EDUCATION.

The design influencer can show how to decorate a table for an alfresco meal with friends with small jars of flowers for a rustic feel, how to create a homemade wreath for your front door, and how to create a peaceful haven for hanging out in a very small space.

The designer can offer INSPIRATION.

The mom can share how to make a box-mix birthday cake look extraordinary by decorating it with fresh flowers and how she manages to keep her stylish house in order with three kids running all over the place.

The mom can offer SOLUTIONS.

STEP THREE: Fill in your grid.

Create a simple grid like mine on a spreadsheet (or use the one below) and start filling in your matrix with general topics that you can cover. Once you've listed the general areas you want to create content around, then you can get more granular and come up with ideas for specific posts. For example, if you look at my matrix, you'll see that "nutrition" is listed under "education" and "luxury lifestyle/dad." Nutrition is a topic from that part of my matrix because I think fitness and wellness are so important. A post inspired by that box in my grid might be about the benefits of intermittent fasting or my favorite new workout.

It's fine if your grid doesn't immediately inspire a dozen ideas for content. The idea is to plot out categories that will serve as a launching pad for more specific ideas that will resonate with your audience and with you. As you're first starting to plan your content, do a quick gut check if you're not absolutely sure a topic fits on your matrix: *Does this make sense for me? Am I getting the right message across?*

The author Mark Manson shares that empathy can be the key to staying on message: "For me, I just try to put myself in my reader or customer's shoes. I ask myself, 'Is this how I want them to feel about me?'" As you're getting creative with your content, think about your audience and how the content will make them feel, and let that information guide you.

CONTENT MATRIX	Character one	Character two	Character three
Offering one			
Offering two			
Offering three			

PLANNING A CONTENT CALENDAR

While a content schedule is exactly that—*a schedule of what content you are going to post and when*—it's not *really* just a calendar; it's a PROCESS that will make your life easier, and don't we all want that? The kind of calendar you use is up to you. There are many online options: Excel spreadsheets, Google Sheets, and old-school paper works too, so if you want to use your Garfield notebook and a purple pen go ahead. The only thing that really matters is that YOU FOLLOW IT. If you're curious, at SER-HANT. we have used ClickUp and Sprout Social, but there are many options out there to explore. Having a process in place *before* you jump into the social media ocean is like getting in with a life jacket that will keep your head above water as you get acclimated. This is how a content calendar will keep you from drowning in the sea of overwhelm:

- You can clearly see what you've posted so you can ensure you're hitting on new topics.
- It promotes accountability, as a big blank space in a content calendar is practically shouting at you to get to work.
- It saves you precious time by making it easier to schedule content in advance.
- You can keep track of everything you've already done, and this helps you find opportunities to repurpose content.

Again, no need to throw yourself headfirst into the ocean. A content calendar will help you ease yourself in!

Fill Out That Calendar with Volume

Trust me when I tell you that your dip into the social media ocean will be smoother if you create content in volume. You don't need to go crazy and plan a year's worth of posts, but having a week's worth of content planned makes it so much easier to stay up to date with your content calendar. I know it can feel intimidating to create content in volume, but there are some tricks to making it doable.

Iman Gadzhi, founder of IAG Media, makes his ultra-busy life easier by using these two tactics: "I repurpose content. We can take a video from YouTube and repurpose it for TikTok. I also have someone who scopes through my iCloud." Again, not everyone can have a content team, but you could hire a savvy college intern to pull good content from your cloud.

Nate O'Brien, the YouTube influencer, suggests, "Work smarter before you work harder. I live by that with everything, even my videos. I'm only going to make a video that's evergreen." Thinking about the longevity of your content while you're planning it can be a way to build your audience base with fewer posts.

Use the 1,000-Minute Rule

Finally, as I always say, USE YOUR MINUTES WISELY. For anyone who read *Big Money Energy: How to Rule at Work, Dominate at Life, and Make Millions*, you know I follow the 1,000-minute rule. After sleeping, eating, spending time with your family, hanging out with your cats—whatever is crucial and important in your life—you have 1,000 minutes left to DOMINATE THE WORLD. I manage my time very, very carefully, and I keep a list in my phone of tasks I can conquer during any unexpected free moments. I save tons of valuable minutes by referring to that list when someone cancels a phone call or a meeting. I don't have to waste a single second figuring out how to use that time wisely. If you're having a slow day, or someone cancels on you, get yourself some caffeine and your favorite snack and have a content creating day!

BRINGING CONTENT TO LIFE

So, what about *writing and producing the actual content*? If the thought of brainstorming ideas, writing, and creating images or videos plummets you into a panic, please let me assure you that you CAN do this. (A major publisher lets me write books! And my social media team does NOT follow me everywhere I go, so I know I am capable of making a good video or taking a good picture.) Push aside that anxiety and forget about results for now. Remember, you are creating social media posts, and while you want to produce good content, you are not trying to win the Pulitzer Prize for literature or the Palme d'Or at the Cannes Film Festival. As you're starting to conceive ideas, think of how you would explain the concept if you were writing an email, or even a text, to a friend or family member. So, if you are a party planner who wants to post content about unique party ideas, think about how you'd explain your concept for an amazing anniversary soiree to your sister. You don't freak out emailing your sister, do you? Sometimes we all need help pulling an idea out of us in order to get it going. Once you get the idea onto the blank screen or onto a blank page, you can adapt the language and select an image that will appeal to the specific audience you want to reach.

Good ideas tend to have minds of their own, and annoyingly they don't always appear when we need them to. If you are being consistent with your content, there's no waiting around for a muse to appear with an armload of wonderful ideas just for you.

When I'm really having trouble coming up with ideas, I'll ask myself, *So, Ryan, what's keeping you awake at night?* Often those pesky thoughts running through my mind about the state of the market, ways to communicate better with clients, different things I can do to inspire my team, and whether it would be weird to wear my favorite tie twice in one week are actually the seeds of an idea. I'll jot them down in my phone and refer back to them when it's time to create a volume of content. I have found that when I am struggling the most creatively, the idea is often right in front of me. . . . *Oh look, I've just spent six minutes in a meeting discussing how important it is to get the hardest task of the day done FIRST THING. Hello, idea!*

Listen, I know you can do this. Clear your mind of any expectations. Don't put any pressure on yourself and forget about the time your ninth-grade English paper came back covered in red marks because your teacher thought it was unimaginative. Start by putting one thought on the page and see where it takes you. As you build your brand and share your thoughts and ideas with your audience, this will start to feel like old hat to you.

How to Create a Video That People Will Actually WATCH

We all know none of that matters if NO ONE WATCHES WHAT YOU POST. We are living in a pressure-filled world where people are consuming content at an insanely fast pace. So how do you get your video about dog grooming to stand out among the thousands of other videos about dog grooming? There is no easy answer to this. (Seriously, if you have one can you please contact me immediately so I can share it with my team? Again, it's ryan@serhant.com.) While there is no magical formula, I can offer some wisdom to help you cut through the noise and give your video of Fido's bath a much better chance. First, get over yourself. You do not need to storyboard this concept or rehearse its execution for hours. LISTEN VERY CAREFULLY. To get people to watch your videos, the videos do not need to be perfect, highly produced,* or directed by Spike Lee (although that would be so cool). Videos need two crucial qualities to succeed on social media. They need to be clean and uncomplicated. CLEAN AND UNCOMPLICATED! That means following these three simple rules:

1. You need to be able to hear the voice of the person who is speaking.
2. You need to be able to see the person's face.
3. You need to be able to see the visuals that need to be seen.

Seriously, this is so important. There is not a high production bar to get into this world, and people quickly forget that and get all caught up in details that don't really matter. A video can be raw and organic and still connect with people. Just follow those VERY BASIC rules and don't let yourself get distracted by the artistry of it all. (If you want to produce an independent film, go ahead, but if you want to get attention for your brand and make more money, this is all you need to do.) And because social media is literally changing as I type these words, CLEAN and

---

* Yes, some of our home tours have a high production value, but that makes sense when you're creating a video to promote an apartment that costs $250 million. This is an EXCEPTION and not the rule, even for me.

UNCOMPLICATED become even more important. Think of those two words as your touchstones as everything changes. . . . Always go back to CLEAN AND UNCOMPLICATED. For example, the runway to launch videos keeps getting shorter. On YouTube you now have fifty-nine seconds *maximum* to tell a story or relay your message. That means there is no room for fluff; there's no room for anything but a clear and uncomplicated message. Always go back to clean and uncomplicated when you're dealing with a social media change. And let's talk for a second about that message you want to send. You have just a couple of seconds to hook your audience, and then the next five seconds will determine if your video will be watched for the NEXT five seconds, and so on. That is less time than it takes to cough. To battle this insane time frame, we use the following formula:

1. **Make an announcement:** Start the video with an announcement of the tactical points that the viewer will take away. When you add a number to the announcement you've informed your audience that there are multiple tips, and knowing that helps string them along.

For example: *Five lessons I learned from a billionaire.*

2. **Share your experience:** I still believe that facts tell and stories sell. And storytelling is the best way to bring my audience into the experience. I think of the story as an ultra-fast sports car that drives the audience straight to the tactical points I'm about to make.

For example: *I was flying in a helicopter to the Hamptons with a billionaire who was on the phone buying a basketball team. And when he hung up, he looked at me and said . . . INSERT BRILLIANT BILLIONAIRE WISDOM HERE.*

3. **The call to action:** After guiding your audience through each point, you need to wrap up the story with a short but powerful call to action that provides a big dose of encouragement to your audience. You aren't just sharing inside information; you're showing how it can HELP. This plants the idea that your content is valuable so that you'll get return visitors.

For example: *To succeed, you must adapt BRILLIANT BILLIONAIRE WISDOM into your life starting NOW.*

Finally, social media is a trial-and-error endeavor, and the sooner you get comfortable with that the better. While you can keep track and measure a video's success, the truth is NO ONE can predict what kind of content will rise to the top. Note what works for you, but you have to stay open to trying, and by focusing on clean and uncomplicated rather than highly produced content, experimentation is possible.

Not long ago I got very excited about the idea of making a longer video about luxury watches for my YouTube channel. I sat down with an expert who looked at my watches and provided some great insight about my collection. (He also made it clear that I should NOT keep my watches stored in an oven mitt.) I really thought this video was entertaining and interesting and would get tons of views. . . . I was wrong. It didn't perform anywhere

PRO TIP: FOLLOW THESE BASICS ABOUT VIDEO PRODUCTION

■ Never position yourself directly in front of a bright light source like a lamp or the sun. If you do this, the result will be a weird, dark silhouette and you'll look like the "anonymous source" who has been blacked out in a true crime documentary. Keep your light sources in front of you and slightly off to the side. A ring light is useful and is a very affordable tool.

■ Keep the eyes of your subject about one-third of the way down from the top of the video frame. Since eyes are the focal point of a person's face, people tend to keep their subject's eye in the center. Unless you have enormous Amy Winehouse hair, this will leave wayyyyyyy too much space above your subject's head.

■ Keep backgrounds uncluttered so that the subject is the main focus. For example, you don't want your audience trying to browse your bookshelves while you're delivering your message.

■ Different platforms have different requirements. These specs are constantly changing, so do some research before shooting your video. It's especially important to know whether the platform utilizes horizontal or vertical orientation, and whether there's a maximum length (but even if there is, don't take it as a sign that you need to make a LONGER video).

near as well as we expected. And yet, a video tour of *my closet* where I showed all my suits and some of my crazy jackets was a huge hit. I had no idea my closet was so interesting, or I would have done a video about it earlier. No matter how carefully you track your successes and no matter how good your content is, social media will still throw you surprises in the form of successes and failures. You have no choice but to roll with those surprises.

KEY PERFORMANCE INDICATORS

Key performance indicators (KPIs) can help you monitor the performance of your posts. You can use this information to determine whether your content is having the desired impact, and to make smart decisions about how to revise your posts.

Reach KPIs

Reach is a measure of how many users come across your social channels and content. Reach data shows your existing and potential audience, your audience growth over time, and your overall brand awareness.

Impressions: The number of times your post was visible in someone's feed or timeline. This does not necessarily mean the person who viewed the post noticed it or read it.

Follower count: The number of followers your social channel has at a set time.

Audience growth rate: How follower count changes over time.

Reach: How many people have seen your post since it went live.

Engagement KPIs

Engagement is a measure of the quality of interactions with your followers.

Likes: The number of times followers interact with your social post by clicking the "like" button.

Comments: The number of times your followers comment on your posts.

Average engagement rate: All the engagement a post receives, including likes, comments, saves, and favorites—divided by the total number of followers on your social channel.

Conversion KPIs

Conversion KPIs measure how many social interactions turn into website visits, newsletter sign-ups, purchases, or other actions.

Conversion rate: The number of users who perform the actions outlined in your social media call to action, or CTA.

Click-through rate (CTR): The percentage of people who viewed your post and clicked on the CTA if it was included.

Engagement Benchmarks to Aim For

When you are getting started you should aim for a 10 percent engagement rate across the board. However, as your reach and follower count grow, refer to the following industry-standard benchmarks:

- **TikTok:** 3–9 percent
- **Instagram:** 4 percent
- **LinkedIn:** 2 percent
- **Facebook and YouTube** are more challenging to quantify in terms of engagement benchmarks because Facebook content is typically shown only to people who opt in to follow a given page, and YouTube engagement relies mainly on viewership, which isn't always easily discoverable.

CONSISTENT, CONSISTENT, AND CONSISTENT

You can follow your content calendar religiously, but if your posts are not in line with your brand messaging you won't connect with the right audience, and *isn't that the point of all this*? Whether you're creating a video about building chicken coops or vintage sneakers, ALWAYS remember that your brand messaging needs to be at the heart of everything you post. Kenneth

Cole, designer and CEO of Kenneth Cole Productions, whose brand has been around for decades so we should absolutely listen to him, emphasizes that staying on brand is crucial to succeed today: "We live in this universal world where everything is available to everybody. Knowledge is literally infinite, and it exists for everybody, so people learn to navigate this universe through brands. If the brand doesn't tell a cohesive, succinct story at every point of contact with the customer, then it doesn't accomplish its objective." In other words, remember that everything you create is another opportunity to *solidify your message* and increase your business just by being consistent.

Consistency is your mantra as you're entering this phase of brand building. Consistency might not sound sexy (it's not the kind of word you'll want to run out and get tattooed on your arm) but consistency is the stuff of life when it comes to building a brand. Not everything about building a thriving business is glamorous and exciting, but what *is exciting* is the huge increase in business and the massive amounts of money that will start raining down if you just stay consistent.

PERFECTIONISM IS YOUR ENEMY, GOOD IS YOUR FRIEND

Finally, please understand this is not the area where you want things to be perfect. Here is one of my early Instagram posts:

> 4:31 a.m. I woke up this morning with so much on my mind. We've started production on #SellItLikeSerhant which is insane. Work is crazy busy. I really really had to pee. But

I was mostly thinking about why I wake up so early. My gut instinct is always to go back to sleep. 1 more hour. 2 more hours. Hell, I'm my own boss. I'm a real estate agent. Maybe I'll just take the day off and watch TV and eat lucky charms! But then I'm always reminded of what my Dad told me when I first came to NYC and got into real estate. I was living at 20 Pine downtown and we were in my living room, and I was complaining about being tired and working all the time and how it wasn't fair. I wanted weekends off. I wanted to sleep. And I wanted my parents to make me feel better and tell me it was all ok and I didn't have to work so hard because I'm such a good boy. And then my Dad cut me off and said, "Stop right there. Do you think that I ever WANTED to wake up early and go to work everyday? No. I WANTED to sleep in. I WANTED to hang out. But that wasn't the job." It may seem weird, but that moment blew my mind. I had always just assumed that my Dad liked waking up at 5:50 a.m. and it was sort of his thing. But the moment he said that to me changed my life. It reinforced that everything we do is a choice. And if you're not making your own choices, then you're someone else's soldier. So get up, get your blood pumping, know your competition at work is still in bed with their blankie, thank God you're alive, and let's #GetIt #READYSETGO

If you're thinking, *Huh, okay. That's fine and everything but you're not exactly blowing my mind with that post, Ryan . . .* know that I agree with you. By the way, I think I got about twenty likes on that one and I was thrilled. I cannot stress this enough: good works. One thing I always like to keep in mind: *good* is subjective. What resonates with you may not resonate with me and vice versa. I think you'd be shocked to learn how many times I'll post something that I think is just okay and then it will proceed to get hundreds of thousands or millions of views because it struck a chord with my audience and even people who have never heard of me before. So don't be a perfectionist. Quality is important and will always have its place in the social media and content creation universe, but more often than not, the person who focuses on volume will beat the person who focuses on quality. Think about it this way—if you're a mob boss trying to rob a bank, would you rather have a team of ten good accomplices or one great accomplice? Sure, having one person that you feel great about may sound nice, but at the end of the day, having ten people helping you plan the break-in, hold up the bank, and carry out the getaway is probably going to get you a lot further.

Also keep in mind that some of the things that are super obvious to you may not be obvious to your followers. Trust me, I get people asking me the same seemingly simple questions all the time. And while the answer feels obvious to me—and thus may feel like there's no point in talking about it in my content—it's a novel concept to many others. For example, I would have never thought in a million years that one of my most popular YouTube videos would be about how real estate agents make money. That video, where I talk about commissions, splits, expenses, and other things I deal with on a day-to-day basis, has received over 14 million impressions and has been viewed over 850,000 times! Yet, if it weren't for my team pushing me to talk about it, I never would have bothered doing so because of how obvious and simple it seemed.

As you build your brand and share your thoughts and ideas with your audience, this will start to feel like old hat to you. And when those platforms you got so used to start to fade away, you'll be ready to embrace that "new family" with open arms. I'm going to stop talking about this so you can get to it. Please! Just treat every post like page one in the book about your life. You have complete control! Think of it as your personal diary if that helps. What if you were abducted by aliens tomorrow? *Wouldn't you be glad to leave your social media posts behind as a legacy of your life that says I WAS HERE!?*

Okay, one last thing. Use the checklists at the end of this chapter to stay organized, don't overthink it, and have fun. Your mission now is to EXECUTE that content!

This chapter is full of information, but you've nailed it all. In this chapter you have accomplished the following:

> Embraced the social media learning curve by being a
>   conscious consumer ✔
> Created your Content Matrix ✔
> Zeroed in on your three characters ✔
> Set up a content calendar ✔
> Created content in volume ✔
> Started to create clean and uncomplicated videos ✔

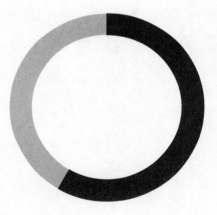

NOW IT'S SYDNEY'S TURN

CONTENT MATRIX

STEP ONE: VISUALIZE YOUR TARGET CUSTOMER AND ANALYZE THE DIFFERENT WAYS THEY SEE YOU.

Character one: Coach

   I'm here to share helpful information that lets you take control of your wellness.

Character two: Busy young professional

   I'm busy too, and I know what it's like to balance prioritizing your health and work.

Character three: Athlete

   I walk the walk AND talk the talk.

STEP TWO: EXPLORE WHAT EACH CHARACTER CAN OFFER YOUR AUDIENCE.

Character one: Coach (EDUCATION)

   I'm here to share helpful information that lets you take control of your wellness.

- Helpful form breakdowns for common exercises
- Tips for building an exercise program
- Advice for working with a personal trainer
- Mic'd up personal training sessions (ME AS COACH)

Character two: Busy young professional (RELATABLE CONTENT)

   I'm busy too, and I know what it's like to balance prioritizing your health and work.

- Day-in-the-life content
- Beat-the-clock routines—how to tap into your productivity
- Productivity hacks

Character three: Athlete (INSPIRATION and MOTIVATION)
I walk the walk AND talk the talk.

- Mic'd up personal training sessions (ME AS CLIENT)
- Clips of my own sessions with my coaches
- Progress tracking against my own goals (e.g., "Train for Hyrox with me!")

STEP THREE: FILL IN YOUR GRID.

	Coach	**Busy Professional**	**Athlete**
Education			
Relatable			
Inspiring			

CONTENT CALENDAR AND PLANNING PROCESS:

1. I've been through the list of free (and paid!) social media planning apps, but I've found the best way to keep myself on track is to keep it simple—I use a spreadsheet or a good old-fashioned pen-to-paper planner.

2. BUT, no matter how much I map my content, staying consistent is always a challenge. Especially when some of my best-performing content requires dedicated time in the gym with a tripod (or a friend) to create.

3. Now I'm trying to find more opportunities to capture content I can repurpose. Whether that's recording more videos during my client sessions (with permission) or participating in content sessions with my Movement & Mindset co-coaches.

WHAT WORKS:

1. Finding the right mix of content for Self by Syd is ALWAYS challenging. I'm trying to create a balance of content that's relatable, fun to watch, inspirational, and encouraging . . . all while showcasing the nuance of my brand against other fitness professionals: I'm busy, I do A LOT of things, so I understand how intimidating—and important—finding a wellness routine that works for you is.

2. Educational video content works best for me: some of my highest performers are video breakdowns of forms and exercise progressions. Inspirational content performs well for Self by Syd, with my Coffee Chat series bringing in significant views compared to other videos.

3. When I started creating content for Self by Syd, it was actually primarily a food account! I was NEVER in frame, let alone talking to the camera. When my own personal goals and journey changed, my content changed—and started performing much better.

4. I'd consider myself to still be in the phase of throwing content at the wall to see what sticks, but I'm at the tail end of it. . . . I see what's performing well and what's underperforming, and becoming more intentional about leaning into that high-performing content will be a game changer for me.

5. If I had a time machine, I'd travel back in time and start creating content with similar editing structures or subject matter to high-performing pieces of content from popular competitive accounts. No sense fixing what isn't broken . . . but it's always important that you add your own authentic viewpoint and voice (and credit where credit is due!).

INSTAGRAM SELF-AUDIT CHECKLIST

The answers should all be YES.

- Do your username, headline, caption, and photograph represent your brand clearly?
- Does your profile represent the person you want to be?
- Is every post on brand? If they aren't, DELETE DELETE DELETE.
- Are you creating stronger connections by responding to DMs?

Which posts have the most engagement (likes and comments)?

What do they have in common?

Which posts have the lowest engagement (likes and comments)?

What do they have in common?

FACEBOOK SELF-AUDIT CHECKLIST

WHO: Who do you want to reach? List target demographics.

HOW: How will you reach them? List content ideas.

Takeaways: What worked and what didn't? Take some time to analyze which aspects of your Facebook posts resonated and which didn't. How can you adjust your content in the future?

YOUTUBE SELF-AUDIT CHECKLIST

Use this list to make sure your YouTube landing page is fully optimized. That means . . .

1. Headshot and banner match existing branding.

2. You've completed the "about" section. This includes a biography. Your bio can be written with personality so it is fun and engaging.

3. You've set up links to your other social media accounts.

4. If you have videos ready to go, they are uploaded and organized into playlists as appropriate.

LINKEDIN SELF-AUDIT CHECKLIST

You can increase your reach by making a commitment to reach out to ten new users Every. Single. Day. Here are some ideas to get you started:

- Colleagues: Connect with others in your industry.
- Professional contacts: Think broadly of people you worked for in the past or had professional interactions with. Go beyond your occupation. Think of other branches of your industry that are connected. For me that could include interior designers, photographers, or mortgage brokers.
- Former classmates: It can be fun to connect with friends. You never know who is going to need the services or products you offer.
- Neighbors/community members: Think of people who are leaders in your community—PTA president, people from your neighborhood HOA, the managers at your daughter's ballet studio, the person you buy bagels from. Connect with your community to see who can potentially help you build your network.

CHAPTER 10

Authenticity: The Key to Long-Lasting Connections

Authentic, authentic, authentic. It seems like that word is everywhere, especially when it comes to talking about personal brands. It wasn't that long ago that the word *authentic* was reserved for statements like, *Look at this amazing Eames lounge chair I got at an estate sale! It's authentic!* And, *If you want to eat some authentic Asian food, there are so many great options in Flushing, Queens. It is foodie heaven!* Or maybe, *Is that bag dangling off your arm authentic crocodile? Are you serious?! No way, it's faux. I respect the reptiles!* While those statements are about whether something is genuine or true, we're talking about furniture, handbags, and finely crafted food. Today, unless you are antique shopping, the words *authentic* and *authenticity* are probably being used to describe influencers, entrepreneurs, celebrities—in other words, brands. *We like Brand X because its billionaire founder/CEO is so authentic. He wears hoodies and sneakers! He's just like me, except with way more money. Miss A-list celebrity is authentic too. She's not afraid to post pictures of herself sans makeup or after a sweaty workout, and I like how open she's been about her struggles with anxiety. Influencer Z, though, with his fancy cars, huge house, stable of racehorses, and private plane . . . When he starts talking about how he loves meditation, it's hard to go along with it. He's so materialistic, and he doesn't seem authentic at all. I mean, the man has an assistant whose only job is to make green juice. Gross!*

Authenticity has become a catchword, and for better or worse it heavily influences how we view brands. At its core, authenticity is about finding the most organic way to forge a strong connection with your audience—and fostering that connection has never been more important for brands than it is today. An authentic connection is simply another way to promote trust and loyalty among customers and clients. The view people get of your authentic self (whether they know it or not) helps them make choices about who they should hire or buy from again and again. *We love our kitchen designer—she's always cooking huge meals for friends on Instagram, and we knew she'd understand how to create a perfect space for entertaining in our home.* Or, *We always get bagels from Sonny's. That place is a fixture in our community. Sonny is so nice, and he always has treats for our dogs.*

I see the irony in analyzing the role authenticity plays in personal branding, but that's just it. You're purposefully building a personal brand, not creating content featuring yourself just for fun. The goal here is to find a natural way *to connect* with new clients and learn to maximize that connection so you are cemented in the heads of your audience as the go-to person in your industry.

On one level it sounds so simple. Just be yourself and everyone will automatically love you for who you are, and you'll create an unbreakable bond that results in years of mind-blowing success for your brand! The truth is, it's not quite that simple. Creating a solid and authentic connection isn't something that happens with one huge success or one viral Instagram post. A long-lasting connection (much like a real-life relationship) develops over time *with consistency*. And it takes work to maintain that connection. Authenticity fuels the flame of that relationship and helps remind the world who you are, what you do, and why your audience should listen to you or even care at all. Think about it: there is a reason we develop deep attachments to brands. Sure, it could be because we love a product or service, but ultimately brands capture our attention in one of several ways—by entertaining us, solving our problems, or providing inspiration. Think of these categories as platforms to let your authentic self shine so that you can connect with your intended audience in a purposeful way.

CONNECTOR 1: THE PUNCH LINE: EARN IT

Not long ago we had an announcement to make about a big development at SERHANT. I was so excited about our news that I had to stop myself from blurting it out to every single person I passed on the street. I even imagined going to the top of the Empire State Building (closest thing we have to a mountain in New York City) with a freakishly large megaphone to shout about this news to all of Manhattan. SERHANT. was going national, and I was so proud that we were making this happen just a couple of years after founding the company. SERHANT. was expanding to New Jersey, Pennsylvania, Connecticut, Florida, and *both* Carolinas. I could have kept things simple and posted about each new territory on our social media accounts like this:

> Me:
>> SERHANT. is now setting up an office in New Jersey!!

I mean, as excited as I was about our growth, I could see that posts like "SERHANT. expands to New Jersey!" or "SERHANT. is coming to Pennsylvania" weren't exactly the most thrilling headlines (well, to anyone other than me and my mother). I worried that a general announcement like that would result in a response like this:

> The entire world:
> SOOOOOOOOOOOO???????????
> Oh! Look at this hilarious video of a dog wearing pajamas! Adorable. I'm reposting this.

Honestly, if I wanted anyone to care about this development and feel connected to my brand at all, I had to go beyond basic and do something to grab people's attention. We had to present this information in such an entertaining way that people couldn't help but take notice. We decided that we would share our news by doing what we do best . . . using media.

We created a video of a fake press conference. I stood behind a podium that had microphones with the logos of leading media networks. Flashbulbs went off as members of my team, who were acting like reporters, shouted out the questions they wanted answered. Standing there fielding questions, wearing a SERHANT. T-shirt under my suit jacket and black sunglasses, made me feel like Tom Brady after a big win! We intentionally made it feel *not quite real*. This added a touch of humor and kept the entertainment factor high. Plus, we weren't trying to fool anyone; we were trying to have fun and get noticed. Our hope was people would think something along the lines of, *Oh look. There's Ryan Serhant doing a press conference! Wait a minute, this is obviously fake . . . but it's really funny, so I'll keep watching this rather than switching over to the thirty-second messy bun tutorial. Oh wow! He's in South Carolina! That's where my parents want to retire! I'll let them know.* Or, *Huh, until just now I didn't know who this guy was, but I have been curious about moving to Florida. I'm going to check out their listings!*

This format also gave me the opportunity to share specific information about our expansion in my own way. My team members shouted out questions like, *Where are you expanding?* (I name the five states.) *Is this a franchise model?* (No.) *Who are your new team members?* (I give them all shoutouts.) And *Ryan, we know you're a fan of* Succession. *Will Zena* [my daughter] *take over the business?* (She's four. Yet to show leadership qualities. The jury is out on that one.) Last, perhaps the most important question of all: *Is this the best time to expand given the state of the economy?* To which I proudly said, "When others pull back, we move forward." I started SERHANT. during a pandemic, when I had no idea if the city would bounce back or if we'd all be fleeing to the countryside to live in our own plastic bubbles. I wanted to remind EVERYONE that we do things differently at SERHANT. We surge ahead while others play it safe, and this is the reason we are the go-to company in luxury real estate. The second anyone in those five states is thinking of buying or selling property, I want them to remember SERHANT. is The Best company to call. I also want other brokerage houses to know we're growing, and to reinforce how well we use media to draw positive attention to all our endeavors.

The response to our video was overwhelmingly positive. We received over half a million views and comments that went above and beyond our usual "that's an amazing property" or "love your commentary on that topic!"–style comments. This time, the comments from construction companies, other brokers, and the heads of business development for major brands were like this:

> "Such a smart video, congrats."
> "LMAO epic way to announce."
> "Now this is some solid content . . . witty and informative! Best wishes, brother!"

Please excuse my outright bragging (I mean, c'mon! Those are good comments!) because I'm sharing this for a reason. We upped the entertainment factor because we wanted to get noticed, get clicks, send a message, create a connection, and be remembered with a powerful "punch line." Ultimately, we were making our presence known in the luxury real estate market by delivering a dose of entertainment by telling the story of our expansion in an unusual way.

Nik Sharma, CEO of Sharma Brands, leans into storytelling frequently with his clients, who have included Hint Water and Milk Bar: "The entertainment angle always works, and it is heavily applicable to nearly any industry. People aren't on social media to see ads—they want to be entertained. When entertainment is the medium to deliver a message, you earn the attention and the right to deliver whatever your punch line is. You tell a story first, but the punch line is the product or service that's being sold." In other words, you're more likely to be listened to if you deliver your message (a.k.a. the product or service) after captivating your audience first.

TELL STORIES WITH PURPOSE

While creating a connection with your audience is about sharing your authentic self (you're not just tossing out random stories because they show "the real you"), you must tell stories *with purpose* so that you can grow your audience, increase your brand visibility, and be insanely successful. If you tell the story about that time you accidentally roller-skated into your neighbor's prize-winning rose bush, destroying it before the big garden show, it needs to provide a pathway to something else that relates back to your brand message. I've told stories about accidentally frying my face in the Mexican sun on a family vacation, looking like a total jerk at an informational interview, doing Shakespeare in the middle of a highway, and having my debit card declined while buying a few dollars' worth of groceries. All true! But there is a point to each of those stories I shared about myself. Those stories were lead-ins to bigger topics like taking control, tenacity, perseverance, and being so scared of failure that I completely changed everything about the way I worked. Those stories provide a look at the authentic me while carrying an important message that supports my personal brand. To ensure you're telling an authentic story that will positively impact your brand, use these guidelines:

1. Know your audience

It isn't any surprise that knowing what your audience wants and needs is essential to building a brand. For storytelling to have maximum impact, put yourself in their shoes for a minute. Who is the person you are trying to reach? Picture them standing in

BRAND IT LIKE SERHANT

front of you and ask yourself, What will motivate this person to click on our video? What kind of tone will they respond to? What are they looking for while they're on their social media accounts? How can we dial up the entertainment factor with our story to get them to keep watching . . . *or, better yet, call their mother and suggest that if they're still planning on selling their house in New Jersey they should be in touch with SERHANT.?* That's the goal. Connect and maintain that relationship by being consistent with your actions, and in the end you'll create more business for yourself.

2. Get emotional

Humans are emotional creatures. We cry, laugh, find joy, and get inspired by all sorts of things. I don't hold back in social media posts when I'm ecstatically happy—that's why you'll sometimes see me leaping onto a countertop (made of the most luxurious Carrera marble in a chef's kitchen, of course) to celebrate a huge sale. I like to share my success; I've worked hard for it, and I truly believe that if I can do it, anyone can. And the declined debit card I just mentioned? When I told that story in my first book, *Sell It Like Serhant,* I didn't hide the fact that I cried on the subway after that experience. It was such a low point! I couldn't afford tofu, one of the cheapest sources of protein around! I'm glad I shared that story, though, and I've been told countless times that my being vulnerable helped people feel better when they were facing a tough time. Work (and life) have many ups and downs, and while I don't recommend daily crying sessions on your social media accounts, don't be afraid to let the real you show. Let your audience celebrate, laugh, and cry along with you. There's an entire spectrum of emotions—feel them all!

3. ABC: Always Be CAPTIVATING!

There are approximately nine billion things on nearly any subject that people can watch at any given time. Cocktail-making tutorials, extreme juggling videos, cute animals, cute *baby* animals, videos about how to make soap . . . *it's never-ending.* So sometimes you have to be brutally honest with yourself. Is this story good enough to capture the attention of my audience? Really? Just because you love it doesn't necessarily mean it can compete with videos about magic tricks and cooking tutorials. Entertainment is subjective, but we always aim to produce the highest-quality videos to get people to interact with us. Whether it's a post of me on vacation in Greece with the family or doing a property tour of a house in Abu Dhabi, the content always needs to be original and fresh and have a clear message. We always ask ourselves, is the point we're making—whether it's about why it's a great time to buy property or how to manage time better—CRYSTAL CLEAR? Finally, when we all ask ourselves, "Would we watch this?" the answer has to be an immediate HELL YES for us to move forward. If we don't feel 100 percent sure that our content can captivate our audience, we ditch it immediately.

CONNECTOR 2: LET ME SOLVE YOUR PROBLEMS

My arm itches like crazy . . . do I have poison ivy? My dishwasher is making an insane noise, and it needs to stop. Is it weird that my second toe is longer than my big toe? I really want to impress my new girlfriend by making her dinner, but I only know how to make pancakes and she's keto. I want to invest my Christmas bonus money, but I have no idea where to begin. A list of typical problems humans regularly face could fill this entire book. And the reason many such problems can be solved instantly (or almost instantly) is because it takes only a few seconds to look up "recipes for people who don't know how to cook and don't eat carbs" on the internet. Before the internet, how society managed to figure things out, like *how to tie a bow tie with a broken arm*, is a mystery because according to a study done by Google, a whopping 90 percent of people go to the internet to solve problems. That's not necessarily a surprise (we all do it all the time!), but it also means that helping people solve problems is a way to authentically connect with your audience and get them coming back to you over and over again.

Daniella Monet, the cofounder of Kinder Beauty and Daniella's Digest, was an animal lover and advocate of animal rights from a young age. Daniella took the leap and adopted an all-plant-based diet when she learned to cook vegan food when her uncle was dying of cancer. This experience ignited a passion and sense of purpose for her. "As much as I want to save animals, I want to save people. It's taken me a long time to lay down these building blocks and build trust on social media, but I can now say I am a solution provider. I've always been conscious about animal rights. It's one thing to eat a certain way, but it's another *to live* a certain way, and beauty is one of the ways animals are sacrificed." Daniella's mission was to help people have balance in their lives pertaining to health and wellness, and she wanted to create beauty products that didn't conflict with these values. "We wanted to provide a solution. We created beauty products that are better for you, better for the planet, with lots of options that are ultimately better for your wallet too." Kinder Beauty's goal is to make it easy for consumers to shop for products that are cruelty-free, vegan, and nontoxic. Now Daniella is viewed as an entrepreneur who is providing *a solution*, creating products, and sharing information with her audience, who are concerned about animals and the planet but still want high-quality lipstick and eyeliner. She's positioned herself as a trusted, friendly, fun, and honest resource for her audience.

Chef Alison Roman views her ability to provide solutions to her audience as a crucial part of what she does. "There's a usefulness and a helpfulness that drives what I do. I feel like I truly live to be helpful, and to have an actual impact on people's lives whether it's through an essay I write that resonates or with a recipe people feel is so solid that they learn it by heart." During the pandemic, when we were all stuck at home, Alison kept on cooking and providing recipes. "People would tell me, *You saved my pandemic.* Or, *You helped me rediscover cooking.* People get very deep and personal with me." Alison isn't just writing recipes; she's consistently showing her audience that she can help them by offering solutions for figuring out what to make for dinner, creating a meal from random pantry ingredients, and baking a dessert that will DEFINITELY impress whomever you are serving it to. It is a testament to her helpfulness that many of Alison's recipes became so popular they are forever known on social media as simply "the dip" and "the cookies."

CONNECTOR 3: INSPIRE ON DEMAND

Have you ever started a big project and instantly regretted it? You had fantasies of having a chic, streamlined wardrobe containing only pieces that look amazing on you. You cleared everything out of your closet and piled it on your bed, and now you have a huge mess, and you are wondering why you didn't just go to brunch with friends instead. Now, the only solution to escape the mess you made is to move to a new apartment (call me!).

Those *I have no idea where to start* moments pop up at the worst times—when we're drafting a presentation at work, decorating a new office, or trying to buy a birthday gift that will put a huge smile on our wife's face. The good news is the internet is AN ENORMOUS GLOBAL REPOSITORY OF IDEAS that can help you figure out how to get started or what to do. But on the other hand, the internet is AN ENORMOUS GLOBAL REPOSITORY OF IDEAS, and you could easily spend the next year of your life searching for the perfect desk chair or looking for ideas about how to organize your pantry. It feels like there are endless options available, and sometimes we need that go-to person to help focus our efforts in a particular direction. Influencers and lifestyle experts give inspiration in the form of moral support or provide carefully curated aspirational images that give us all something to aim for or give us a fresh perspective. Athena Calderone, best-selling author, cook, interior designer, and stylist, who recently launched a namesake collection with Crate & Barrel, has inspired people by sharing all aspects of her chic and elegant lifestyle on EyeSwoon. What originally started as a Tumblr to share tips and recipes with friends as she decorated her own home has grown into a trusted source for home decor, style, entertaining, and cooking inspiration. "EyeSwoon was a way for me to build a community, learn, and share. I have always wanted to be the student and the teacher. To this day, EyeSwoon remains an avenue for me to self-educate and share what I've learned along my journey." Athena had developed a strong connection with her audience by communicating "the whys" behind her design choices. "I don't want to just share a beautiful image and say, 'Look at this aspirational picture!' I want to distill it down to the actionable principles at play so that people can learn something. I want people to feel like, 'I get it now. I get why she played with asymmetry in that vignette.' I want to share the why and the how behind the beautiful design."

Influencers who provide inspiration are like role models in a way. Seeing how someone else conquered a challenge (turned a disaster of a closet into a brag-worthy Pinterest post) or succeeded (started a successful business in their parents' basement) can help us tap into our excitement and find a boost of energy to get us to the next step. Seeing how someone else renovated a kitchen with their own two hands serves as proof that *it is* possible. Being that source of possibility can motivate others, provide confidence, and give people the sense that they're being supported in their endeavors (even if there is zero real-life connection). Sharing those inspirational messages, aspirational images, and stories will draw like-minded people your way, positioning your personal brand as a valued resource.

PRO TIP: FORGET ABOUT BEING PERFECT

While people respond to attractive and aspirational images, let's be honest—social media often presents a distorted view of reality, with people showcasing only The Best moments of their lives. Being authentic on social media means being okay with not being perfect at all times. Of course, we want to highlight our wins and showcase our best selves, but people want to see the pared-down you too. The iconic designer Rebecca Minkoff has experienced the positivity that comes from sharing some of those rawer moments. "It can be a tough balance. People want glossy, perfect, and pretty but with the realness of an actual human. A great example of this is a reel we put on my Instagram. I'm just walking with a baby and carrying a tote, and I'm not necessarily looking especially pretty. That reel got more views than any brand content we've done in the last year." While Rebecca's Instagram still features beautiful pictures of her looking like a glamorous New Yorker, dressed up and carrying one of the handbags she designed, there are also glimpses of who she is when she's not at work—a wife and a mother of four—and it's a powerful, likable combination. Embracing your imperfections, or just authentic, real-life moments, can make you more relatable and help you connect with others on a deeper level.

AUTHENTICITY

Right now, when I look at my wrist, I see the rose gold Daytona Rolex that I impulsively bought at an airport in Miami (because I could). I have a few other watches now, but this one has special meaning. I explained in *Big Money Energy* that when I first started out, I associated Rolex watches with massive success. I thought buying a fake one would help boost my confidence. It did for a while, but I let it go when my wrist turned green, and I had more faith in my own capabilities by then anyway. I've always made a point to share my true self on social media, but when I revisited this story in greater detail, I admit I felt nervous. Would I come off as pathetic? Materialistic? Or, oh my God, WOULD PEOPLE QUESTION WHETHER EVERYTHING I OWN IS FAKE FROM NOW ON? WOULD I BE ACCUSED OF DYING MY HAIR GRAY JUST TO LOOK MORE MATURE? I didn't expect that my confession would become one of our most popular posts of all time. Even better, no one made fun of me or called me out on my blatant period of UN-authenticity. People appreciated my honesty and understood why the fake watch was helpful to me, leaving comments like "I needed this today" or "that totally makes sense."

Sharing your real thoughts, feelings, and experiences strengthens the bond between your personal brand and your core audience. Ironically, the popularity of that video reminded me how much authenticity matters. It confirmed that when I shared stories about my journey to where I am today (sometimes embarrassing and verging on pitiful), people feel inclined to connect. I'm not some polished real estate broker who followed a rainbow to a massive pot of gold that was waiting for me inside of a luxury penthouse. I've gone through all of the same challenges, doubts, and fears that we all experience when building a brand and a business.

We all experience great moments and some *less than great ones* that make us want to hide under a blanket. No matter where you are on your personal journey to success—embrace everything that makes you YOU. Toss that blanket aside, get up, and know that the real-life humanness of you matters. We don't need to obsessively hide our flaws or feel ashamed of mistakes. Open up, share your truth, and enjoy all the connections you make along the way. Being authentic in every aspect of your life just might play a role in making all your dreams come true. I know it is something that has helped me on my path to success; all I have to do is look at my wrist—the one with the real rose gold Rolex—to know that the real me makes a difference.

You have taken so many great steps in this process. In this chapter, you have accomplished the following:

> Determined which kind of Connector you are ✔
> Learned to tell stories with purpose by:
> Knowing your audience ✔
> Using ABC: Always Be Captivating ✔

NOW IT'S SYDNEY'S TURN

I related to two key connector areas:
CONNECTOR 2: Let me solve your problems

The essence of Self by Syd is to solve the problem of information overload by putting your health back into your own hands. Because of that, much of my content surrounds the idea of offering new perspectives or new ways to approach finding solutions.

CONNECTOR 3: Inspire on demand

Everyone who has started and stopped a new pursuit in health and wellness can relate—feeling inspired is CRUCIAL to getting you through those tough moments when motivation is running on empty. My content not only provides that inspiration to spark motivation but also provides the inspiration that feeling healthier and happier is attainable for us all.

CHAPTER 11

TMI and Other Ways to Instantly Ruin Your Brand

There's another important reason why we need to be consistent with our messaging while building a brand. You've put so much work into creating your personal brand, and it's important to protect what you've built. Straying too far from your brand personality or brand values on social media can result in a Very. Regretful. Post. Luckily, I learned this lesson without too much regret.

There was a period in my life when every single time I looked into the mirror I sighed sadly, *Yep, there's still a tomato-red acne face staring back at me.* I struggled with acne and rosacea for a long time, and it decimated my confidence. It would be years before I finally got it under control. In the early days of social media, I decided I would write a post about how I conquered this problem (with pictures from my red-faced period). I also included my skin care routine that took ages to perfect (the trial and error included one extra-harsh treatment that made my entire face peel off). I thought being open and vulnerable and sharing would be helpful. I thought I couldn't be the only person who has a problem that is gnawing away at their self-worth.

After the post went live, I sat back and waited for the comments to roll in. The first responses I got caused me almost as much embarrassment as my skin did. Comments ranged from "Whoa, not sure we need an in-depth, play-by-play commentary on your pimples, dude!" to simply, "HOW GROSS." Scrolling through the comments, shame spread over me like a bad rash. *What was I thinking, advertising my skin problems to the entire world? Who does that? And great, now every time someone sees me on TV, they're going to think of me as the Pimple Broker. Who would want to buy an apartment from that guy?* Just as I was thinking about giving up on everything and moving to the middle of Montana, more comments came in:

> "I have had this problem too. Glad you shared."
> "It's always nice to know that someone on TV isn't perfect!"
> "I need more information, please tell me EVERYTHING you did."

This was when social media was still new, and being raw and vulnerable in posts wasn't exactly the norm. It was still entrenched in a more *show everyone how amazing you are* phase. I am lucky that my skin post didn't turn into a regretful embarrassment, and I am glad plenty of people appreciated my openness, but it taught me to think twice (or three or four times) in the future before posting anything that could be perceived as TMI.

We've all felt The Cringe—that uncomfortable-all-over feeling you get after you've seen something you can't unsee or you've read something so ick-inducing that you'll never be able to think about the person who posted it in the same way EVER again. Did any of us really need to know that Megan Fox doesn't flush the toilet, Ashton Kutcher never shuts the door when he goes to the bathroom, and Chrissy Teigen had armpit liposuction? No, we did not. TMI, as we all know, stands for Too Much Information, and while it's best avoided, knowing *how* to avoid it is complicated. Whether or not a topic falls squarely into TMI territory depends on so much: the topic itself, your audience, and what your audience has come to expect from your brand's personality. While posting a story about getting drunk and throwing up all over your prom date may result in a TMI for some personal brands, for other brands it is just another funny story that will yield comments like, *Oh man, my friends and I drank peppermint schnapps at my prom, and we all got so sick. . . . My dad didn't let me borrow his car again for another year! I lost the deposit on my tuxedo too.* There is a huge range between what is acceptable and what results in your embarrassing post being shared a billion times while the entire world comments about how gross you are.

Unfortunately, when it comes to brand building, feeling embarrassed by a TMI moment is the least of your problems. A TMI incident can result in damage to your reputation, loss of trust, and alienating your audience, and it can negatively impact your potential to forge partnerships, collaborations, and promotional opportunities. It takes only the click of a button for someone to unsubscribe, and it takes only one follower with a large audience to post something negative about your brand that could have a wide-reaching impact.

While it is very difficult to know where the line between pushing boundaries and TMI actually is, you can establish protocols to help your personal brand avoid TMI backlash. To reduce the chances of your audience unsubscribing en masse after an ill-conceived post, you need to have criteria for determining what content aligns with brand values and matches your brand personality. You need to get clear about what is considered on or off the table for your personal brand.

PRO TIP: USE COMMON SENSE

It really boils down to this: If it MAKES SENSE for your brand to be talking about sex, gastrointestinal issues, dental work, popping pimples, etc., then it probably isn't TMI. However, if the potentially embarrassing/gross/offensive topic has NOTHING to do with your brand—avoid it.

WHAT'S ON YOUR TABLE?

It is important to establish what is okay to share and what should stay behind the scenes so you can keep your personal brand in the best light. Knowing what's on and off the table for me is always at the forefront of our planning. It helps us maintain the appropriate tone and directs us to the right topics, so we don't accidentally tip into TMI territory. I also make sure any content aligns with my brand values and the tone of my posts meshes with my brand personality. That means posting pictures of myself sweaty and in my gym clothes is a yes for me, because health and fitness is important to me and something I talk about a lot. Anything exercise related fits in well with my personal brand, so I'm okay with posting videos at the gym with my hair all crazy under my headband . . . *because I'm working out.* What I wouldn't post is a picture of me half asleep on the couch, desperately trying to stay awake because the finale of *Succession* is on, and *I know* if I don't watch it ASAP someone is going to ruin the ending for me. Of course I watch television! But television watching isn't a part of my brand, and no one is going to be inspired to hire me to sell their Hamptons estate because they saw a post of me semi-passed out watching TV.

While brand personality and brand values are the best guide to determine what's on the table and what's off, what you post is STILL such a personal thing. What is a YES for a brand that is described as contractor AND rodeo champion versus attorney AND activist can look totally different. Topless bull riding can be appropriate for that contractor, but people might prefer their attorneys to appear a bit more buttoned up. No matter what you do for a living, you need to establish what is on and what is off the table for your brand NOW. You shouldn't be hovering over the post button, asking yourself, *Well, I'm known as the number one college application consultant, so everything about my personal brand is going great! I wonder if my audience will enjoy this post about my passion for mud wrestling. Probably, right?* Save yourself by thinking about this before you step into scalding water with no way out.

Ryan's Table

Family posts are on my table, but I always run them by Emilia first. She has full veto power. Zena is in many of my posts, and I love sharing her adorableness with the world, but I realize that those days could be numbered. As she grows up, I will ask her

BRAND IT LIKE SERHANT

if she wants to be on my social media, and if she declines I will have a strict NO ZENA policy. It only seems fair. I certainly don't want her posting videos of me brushing my teeth on her Instagram without my permission.

On the table:

- Ryan in the office
- Ryan in the car (which is also my office, just on wheels)
- Ryan on the streets of New York City
- Ryan in apartments
- Ryan with family
- Ryan at work-related events
- Ryan working out
- Stories about how I grew as a businessperson, developed confidence, and found my path

Off the table:

- Ryan watching TV, or generally lounging around adding nothing to the world.
- Detailed personal financial information. Too much!
- Random day-to-day moments at SERHANT. (I show plenty of things, but a lot of what I do is really, really boring. Also, some clients and team members are not keen to be on my social media feed, which is completely understandable.)
- Eating, especially junk food. I know I shared my love for Doritos in this book, but I'm not going to make a TikTok about the wonders of Lucky Charms.

Adjust Your Table Settings Accordingly

I do try to stay open (just a little bit!) to adding things to my table, even just temporarily, and I've been pleasantly surprised (and massively relieved) by the results. Talking about my own privilege and personal finances makes me queasy. I'm all for celebrating success, but I never want to come off as bragging or showing off. I recently opened up the door just a crack on a new topic, and I have to admit that at first I was TERRIFIED. I shared that I came from a fortunate background and that I felt privilege was something that can come and go. Long story short:

- I had supportive parents. Dad had a good job, I got to try out sports and activities, and I had a magic set and access to my favorite Jell-O pudding. We had a nice home. My parents paid for an excellent education. Ryan Serhant was set up for success!

- Moved to New York City to become an actor, was on my own financially in one of the most expensive cities in the world, lived in a horrible apartment that was all I could afford, and dealt with a ton of rejection day after day in auditions. But I can't say I was flying completely without a net. Finances were precarious, money scarce, food insecure, but I knew, as humiliating as it might be, or as crushing as it might feel, if worse came to worst I could move back home with my parents, so I wasn't going to be homeless. That's a privilege.

- I had no money (and didn't want to move home) so I made a pivot to real estate—hello, and good luck living off the $9,000 you earned in your first year! Time to work much harder. Make sure you get up earlier every morning to get in line for the shower in the bathroom that you share with about twenty other people.

- Worked harder, still lived in that apartment with a few large cockroaches as my roommates, made more money. I could buy groceries without trying to calculate the total in my head as I shopped! My debit card was no longer declined. Things were looking up all around.

- Repeat pattern. Increased benefits that allowed me to become even more successful came in the form of an assistant, money in the bank, and an apartment with my own bathroom, and it just kept leading to my life becoming less difficult and more comfortable as I continued to work really hard and appreciate every single thing I had.

I want to make the point that while you *can't* change your circumstances, you can work hard and earn a lifestyle that wasn't initially accessible to you. You can earn the luxury of freedom to determine where you work, how long you work, what you do, and who you surround yourself with. Of course, it's true that some people start out with a lot more privilege than others, whether that be financial, racial, educational, geographical, having a loving support system, etc. That's a fact we can't ignore.

I wanted to express that most of us have at least some level of privilege, even if it's minimal, like living in a house or having food to eat, and we can use one privilege to build on another. I'm ultra-privileged, especially now (and yes, privilege certainly doesn't eliminate the fact that you need to work extremely hard in this life for what you want), and I was scared about how this post would be perceived. Did the meaning of my message land? Or should I just leave work right now and get "privileged white guy" tattooed on my forehead? Thankfully I remain tattoo free. The responses were overwhelmingly positive. I was thanked for opening up about my journey and being honest about my own path, acknowledging what I came to the table with and how I built on that so I could keep growing and evolving. I wasn't successful just because I was privileged. I was successful because I acknowledged what I had and what was working for me, I made a hard pivot when things weren't working out for me the way I wanted, and I kept reevaluating and evolving and I worked hard. If I hadn't done those things, my privilege would have been pretty meaningless, and I'd be doing local theater back home and living in my childhood bedroom, asking my mom to put chocolate pudding on the grocery list.

I would still say that posts about my finances remain largely off the table. The difference here was that the message of *you do have some control over your life and some of us have more privilege than we think we do* was directly tied to my feelings about hard work and success. There was a clear reason why I was willing to adjust my table settings: the post about my privilege was adjacent to success, and success is something that absolutely meshes with my brand values and personality. What you put on your table is up to you, but it's a worthy endeavor to think about how you can rearrange your table from time to time. It can show a new side of you and bring your personal brand and your audience closer together.

PLACES THAT ARE EASY TO GO

While there is never going to be an easy-peasy, yes-or-no answer across the board, there are topics that increase transparency and tend to be viewed favorably by nearly everyone. There is no limit to topics that can be talked about in social media posts, but there are a few "safe" places to go that inspire and promote connection, so go ahead and talk about the following in a way that is in line with your brand values and personality:

1. Money

Unless you live off the grid and hunt for all your food and have built a house out of trees you felled yourself, we ALL NEED MONEY TO LIVE. Posts about getting it and hanging on to it are appealing to nearly everyone. Whether your brand is new and you're in the struggle phase or you're a CEO earning seven figures, the topic of money (and how to get it) consistently sparks curiosity. While I've just spent a good portion of this chapter explaining that this is not a comfortable area for me, I remain very curious about how money works for everyone else!

Potential areas to cover: How much money a person or a business makes (TMI *for me* but it's game on for many people), how exactly the money is made, how the business got started, how much money was there to work with in the beginning, the ins and outs of working with investors, overcoming financial obstacles, mistakes that are easy to make, and how to navigate the ups and downs that nearly every business faces. This is just helpful information on how a business is created, how it runs, and how it grows, and people will appreciate it. It's an education, not a brag.

2. Relationships

Assuming you don't live alone in a tree house high in the canopy above the rainforest, navigating relationships is something we do every single day. Our families, partners, kids, dating lives, inter-actions with colleagues and bosses, and friendships are impor-tant relationships that have a huge impact on our happiness and ability to succeed. Knowing how to avoid problems and keep-ing these relationships positive and healthy is a draw for many people.

Potential areas to cover: Dates gone horribly wrong, what never to do on a date, what you should always do on a date, being ghosted, how to create the best dating profile, how to let someone down easily, how our wonderful parents set us up for success (thanks, Mom and Dad!), how our awful parents set us up for failure and how we overcame that, lessons learned from parents, what we've learned as parents ourselves, what to do when your partner thinks you work too much, how to have the best date night ever, friends who've got your back, toxic friends you need to excise from your life, how to make friends as a busy adult, how to deal with annoying colleagues, the boss who steals your ideas, the boss who won't give you a promotion or raise, how to be a good boss, the ultra-supportive boss who changed your life by giving you the world's greatest advice.

3. Health and Wellness

Most of us are on a never-ending quest to be our best selves. We want healthy skin that glows as bright as a sunbeam, shiny hair, a strong physique, and a positive mindset. Topics that feature information on how to be a better person, both physically and mentally, are eaten up.

Potential areas to cover: Before-and-after journeys, skin care routines (so now it's acceptable to talk about your zits!), mindfulness, meditation, how to sleep better, workout routines, recipes for green juices and protein shakes, salads that are made of superfoods, gut health, workout gear, gratitude, what to eat and what not to eat, how to squash cravings for sugar, cleanses, developing healthy habits, the power of getting up early (I love this one), clean makeup, beauty routines, and self-acceptance.

PLACES TO ENTER WITH CAUTION

Politics, sex, and religion. These areas are as gray as a late February sky. Brands all over the spectrum have had great success including these topics, but the opposite is true too! There is nothing inherently wrong with any of these topics, but different people have different views on these things, and it can cause unnecessary conflict and bad reactions, so you need to think about whether it makes sense for you to go here.

Politics

If your personal brand has nothing whatsoever to do with politics, there's no real need for you to discuss your political beliefs. Sharing your political beliefs will likely result in part of your audience liking you a lot more, and part of it liking you a lot less. Think of this as a net negative for your brand. However, if you run a nonprofit dedicated to securing affordable health care for women, for example, then it's a different story. Sharing your beliefs will be a quick way to get you in front of your target audience.

Religion

Like politics, this can go either way. While questions and conversations about faith and spiritual insights appeal to plenty of people, talking about your beliefs, what you specifically believe, or if you don't believe can be divisive. If you decide to go here, be respectful of the views of others.

Sex

There are plenty of people who talk about sex openly, and it works well as part of their brand. The question again is, does this make sense for YOU? Sex can make great content, of course, but you've got to be extra aware of crossing that line into TMI territory.

DANGER!! DO NOT ENTER!!!

What brands stand for and what they give back to society have never been more important. There's a strong desire from consumers for brands to be "good." Tom Bilyeu, founder of Quest Nutrition, aptly points out, "If you have the business acumen, but you are a dick, odds are you're in trouble because people are going to suss you out pretty fast. We are fortunate to be living at a time when the best marketing vehicle's being a good person and doing the right thing." What this boils down to is simple: don't be a dick. Avoid stepping in bullshit with the following kinds of posts because that shit can follow you around FOREVER:

The lie: Truth always wins. If you are making yourself out to be richer, more successful, and more generous than you actually are, you are sending a specific message to your audience, and that message is, *You can't trust me, and my brand is built on lies.* Exaggerating about your achievements or sharing bullshit stories about that time you ran with the bulls in Spain or invented a new element for the periodic table will come back to bite you. Hard.

The vent: The big, wide world of TikTok and Instagram does not exist to serve as your personal therapist. No one needs an in-depth, play-by-play report of why your life sucks, your parents suck, your job sucks. Save your stories about what sucks in your life for your own therapist. Sucking is not a brand.

The faux expert: It is possible to be very well versed in certain subject matter without having official qualifications. I'm not a nutritionist, but I've talked about why I like intermittent fasting! But I don't pretend to have a master's degree in nutrition and dietetics! Share what you've learned, share personal experiences, talk about "what's worked for me," but don't pretend to have credentials that you don't have.

The call out: The internet is not a place to air your grievances about other brands, companies, or people. Someone skipped you in line at Starbucks? No need to share that with your audience, even if you are bursting with outrage. Someone in your life has totally wronged you? Call them to discuss it; don't post about it. Our mothers were right when they said tearing people down is not how you build yourself up. This is how you look like a dick. And please, do not Kanye West yourself. I certainly hope you're not harboring any prejudice or hatred for specific groups, and if you are, keep it to yourself (and seriously, get some help, please!).

READ THE ROOM

While being authentic is one thing, being an insensitive jerk is another. There are times and occasions where it is essential to read the room and adjust your brand personality accordingly. I don't swear when I talk on the phone to my grandmother in Wisconsin, and I don't feel I am inhibiting my authentic self by doing that. Tom Bilyeu explains how he makes slight adjustments when the room calls for it: "I go live on my Discord community once a week, and I'm different there. It's a smaller group; it's more intimate. One of the guys listening was like, 'You're less guarded in here.' I thought that's true. It's me, but I'm always contextual. I gave a talk in Dubai at a government forum, and I decided I'm not going to swear, not a single word. That's not my normal thing. Swear words are spicy; I like them. But in that context, it felt disrespectful. I never want to say something that isn't true. I never want to say something that isn't authentic, but I'm thoughtful about who I'm speaking to in the moment."

Don't risk taking a hit on your personal brand in the name of authenticity. Read the room. Know who you are talking to, know what's appropriate and what should be avoided, and adjust yourself accordingly. You can use as many swear words as you want later.

There were times when I was writing this chapter that I felt like I should be wearing a T-shirt that read CAPTAIN OBVIOUS in big, bold letters. All these concepts should come across as common sense and basic courtesy, but posting something regretful can take a few seconds and there you are . . . back at sad, lonely square one with a tainted personal brand because you posted something you shouldn't have in a heated moment. We are all human; we are all prone to anger, frustration, confusion, and general WTF? moments. We have those days when people skip us in line at Starbucks and it's no big deal, then we have days where a slight like this fills us with rage. Don't let any of your normal human emotions dictate your actions. Don't let a bad day or dark moment infect everything you post. Be aware of your actions no matter how you are feeling.

We have never before had access to a tool as powerful as social media. Have fun out there, but be careful, be mindful, and proceed carefully when planning your content. When your Spidey sense tingles in a *maybe I shouldn't be doing this* kind of way, LISTEN TO IT. A regretful action can go from an *oops! I shouldn't have said that* to the utter destruction of your personal brand in the time it takes to refresh your feed. Remember all this, and you'll never have to start over.

Hopefully this chapter will help you avoid TMI situations. This is what you've accomplished in this chapter as we wrap up Phase Two: Consistency Is Key:

Decided what is ON your table ✔
Decided what is OFF your table ✔
Learned about safe and unsafe content areas ✔

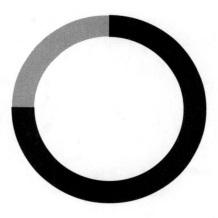

NOW IT'S SYDNEY'S TURN

TMIs—WHAT NOT TO SHARE

1. Before-and-after content that features ONLY aesthetic results. Wellness is more than what your body looks like.
2. Specific workouts (e.g., full-body workouts, ten-minute workout to train your upper body, etc.). For the record, I think these are fine, and I used to post workouts! But I've grown to understand how this type of content can be taken out of context or leveraged by the wrong audience. Instead, I'd share content about how to craft your own exercise program with elements that are specific to your goals and capabilities, or something like "Tips for Finding Your Next Personal Trainer."
3. Content that blatantly knocks another person for their choices. I've seen way too many content creators in fitness share content with clips of people doing silly things at the gym, or lifting with poor form, or making fun of someone's eating habits. Any time I want to post a more critical piece of content, it's always assessing MY OWN old videos, and it always comes from a place of education first.

PHASE THREE:

Shout It from the Mountaintop

CHAPTER 12

The Power of Amplification

Even the most polished personal brand won't thrive if no one has heard about it, and a single person can make only so much noise. Sure, you can yell and scream all you want about why your brand is the go-to for custom tennis rackets or you are the best wedding planner alive. Making noise is *very* important, but doing it all on your own isn't sustainable. Even the most energetic of toddlers throwing the loudest and most epic tantrum will eventually give up and pass out for a long nap, exhausted by the effort. You can't waste your precious time up there on a mountain screaming at people who won't listen to you. So, before you climb up onto that mountaintop to get attention for your brand, you need to create a strategy so that your hard work yields results.

I was fortunate enough to learn this *on the ground* before I strapped myself into a harness and started that big ascent. In my early New York City days, I couldn't afford a gym membership. When I struck a deal with a local gym to pass out flyers in exchange for a free membership, I felt like I had struck gold. *I just need to hand these out to people so they'll be aware of this great gym? So easy!* I set myself up on a busy street corner. I was full of energy and confident in my ability to enlighten my fellow New Yorkers about this exciting new gym. READY, SET, GO! I psyched myself up and put a big smile on my face as someone approached. *Hi! Do you know about this gym? They're offering specials and here's a fl—* Before I could finish my sentence, I was cut off with a loud "NO" by a harried mom pushing a stroller who glared at me like I was a kidnapper. *Oh, okay, well, she looks busy.*

That abrupt NO would turn out to be the closest I got to having an actual interaction with someone. Dozens and dozens of people walked past me, and no one would look at me. It was as if I didn't exist! *Hmm, I added a new protein powder to my smoothie this morning; could it have rendered me invisible?* I stood there desperately willing people with my mind to Take. A. Flyer. *Take it take it take it why won't anyone take it?* I'm asking people to take a piece of paper, not donate a kidney! Finally, a few people took them, but they all looked really angry about it, like I had handed them a bag of warm dog poop. I saw one man crumple up his flyer and throw it in the trash right in front of me. *Could he not have waited until he hit the next block to throw it away?* What sounded so easy felt so hard. I couldn't get anyone to listen to me for three seconds.

I noticed a friendly-looking older man with a dog approaching. I took a deep breath and decided to give it one last go. *Hi, there's this great new gym that's opened and here's some info.* I outstretched my hand with a flyer. The man stopped. Finally! I did it! But then he spoke. "Who the hell are you, and why should I listen to you about joining some gym?" He gave me a dirty look (I swear his dog did too) and went on his way.

I could have stood there for the rest of my life. I could have been louder, more forceful, but no one was paying attention to me. Maybe if I was Arnold Schwarzenegger people would have been compelled to learn about the gym, but I was just some random guy on a street corner with a stack of paper. I had zero credibility. I started to think about it. *Why should anyone listen to me?* For all anyone knew, maybe I had never exercised in my entire life, and it could be the worst gym ever. Or maybe this "new gym" didn't even exist, and I was actually trying to lure people into an illegal underground gambling ring. There was nothing about me or my pitch to indicate that my message was worth listening to. Thankfully, the stakes were not high for me. I wasn't required to get X amount of people to join the gym in order for me to keep working out there. But I did get an early lesson about how you need to establish some credibility if you want to get someone to listen to your message or hold their attention.

THE THREE C'S: CREDIBILITY, COVERAGE, AND COMMUNITY

Ultimately, shouting from the mountaintop is about amplification. **You don't amplify by making more noise; you amplify by establishing credibility, getting coverage of your brand, and creating a community around your brand.** Instead of shouting until your throat is raw, you build partnerships and alliances so that you have a chorus of people echoing the same sentiments, amplifying the volume of your message many times over. I like to think of this process as building a self-fueling publicity machine that will let the world know YOU are the BEST . . . ON REPEAT.

CREDIBILITY: THE CRUCIAL STAMP OF APPROVAL

I possess an insane amount of knowledge about real estate. I can rattle off the average price per square foot of every neighborhood in Manhattan, give you tips on how to get approved by the toughest co-op boards, and tell you what buildings have the nicest doormen, how much your dog has to weigh to be allowed to live in building X, and what the latest record-breaking sale was in Florida. I am not the only broker who knows all this, but I am one of a handful who are asked to go on television, provide quotes for magazine and newspaper articles, and give speeches all over the world. It's not that I'm the self-appointed all-knowing king of real estate; it's that I made a deliberate plan to establish my credibility as I built my brand. There are three ways to do this: thought leadership, speaking engagements, and awards.

TRANSFORMING THOUGHTS INTO
THOUGHT LEADERSHIP

You become a thought leader when your commentary is viewed and valued by your peers. Providing industry commentary can sound challenging, but chances are you are already doing this informally, practically every day, and you don't even realize it. Say you're an interior designer and you're having coffee with a friend in your field. After your matcha latte arrives, you sigh, *You know what's weird? Everyone wants an open floor plan! Why are people obsessed with living in one giant room? Don't people understand they'll have to listen to their kid practicing the recorder while they're trying to unwind with a book and a glass of wine? And* behold, that is the seed for some industry commentary that you can use to boost your brand. Those thoughts can be channeled into a blog post or a LinkedIn article called "Five Reasons We Need to Stop with the Open Floor Plan." You have thoughts about your business all the time! Your ideas and opinions can be channeled into useful information for other people in your field or people who use the product or service you offer. Thought leadership also leads to "coverage," which we'll get to soon. Journalists are going to check you out before they deem you a good resource for quotes, so having articles you've crafted on LinkedIn is evidence for journalists that you know what you're talking about. As I'm thinking of new ways to spin thoughts into thought leadership, I use the following tactics to guide me:

Five Ways to Share Thought Leadership

1. **Lean on your AND.** Think of your AND as a secret ingredient that can help your viewpoints stand out. For example, I wrote an article for *Forbes* about "why real estate agents need to embrace the metaverse." Since I am luxury real estate AND media, I can offer a unique perspective on why the metaverse can be a useful tool for brokers.
2. **Be an outlier.** If you have an idea or opinion that is off the beaten path, share it! Bringing fresh insights out in the open is another opportunity to differentiate yourself. In my world, no one wants to read the same old boring stuff like "how to improve your curb appeal." What could get attention is "gardens are the new lawns:

stop mowing and start planting flowers." *Wait, what? People don't want GRASS?! Okay, I'm listening!*

3. **Dare to predict.** What's going on in your industry right now, and where will it take things? During the height of the pandemic, many people were leaving New York City, and I was wondering if I'd need to transfer my real estate license to the moon. Around that time, I was asked to appear on the Neil Cavuto show on Fox News. When we were talking about the state of the industry, and how GRIM it all seemed with the pandemic, I suddenly had an epiphany: *"NO! I'm not betting against New York!"* I talked about how New York City always survives and nothing could keep it from bouncing back—even a pandemic. Neil thought I was crazy and just plain WRONG. I remember he looked at me like, *Oh, you're so wrong, and I just feel bad for you.* A year later, when it was clear that I WAS RIGHT and the market was heating up again, I had the opportunity to go back on the show. "You know when you were here last year? You really called it. You were right." This appearance wasn't just media attention. My contrary position reinforced that my brand personality is limitless and successful.

4. **The unique fact technique.** I always have one unique fact memorized that I can refer to during an interview. Knowing I have this fact in my back pocket feels better than having a good luck charm that's made of rainbow dust and has been blessed by a unicorn. I can use this fact to pivot a conversation if I need to. I am always

glad to be on TV; however, I prefer talking about my current brand and the business I'm doing rather than talking about my experiences on reality television. (I'm grateful! It's just . . . what about that sales record I just broke? Can we pleeeease talk about that?) My unique fact gives me a way to politely pivot away from a topic to one that shows me in a good light and puts control of the narrative back in my court. Your fact should connect to your brand, be memorable, and shed new light on a topic. To quickly sum up my favorite fact of late, *While interest rates in the '80s were notoriously high, ultimately, if you look at changes in the cost of the average home and salaries today, you'll see that our spending power has changed dramatically, making it more difficult for people to enter the housing market today.* This fact has data to back it up, isn't something that's often discussed, and can immediately change the direction of a conversation.

5. **The rule of five.** I admit I use the rule of five all the time, which is when you come up with a list of five things to focus on for your reader when writing a blog post, article, or social media post. It's something that people can absorb and use easily and doesn't require them to read through a long article. Lists of "rules of five" grab attention. I've used it for articles like "five creative ways to beat the summer slump" and "five things to expect from home inspections." Content like this is efficient, and a reader can fly through it quickly. When every minute of our lives is a barrage of content,

this makes your article more appealing. Promising five tips also tells readers right away that they're going to get easy and actionable suggestions that can be put to use immediately. It's like a bonus call to action.

HA. DO YOU SEE WHAT I DID THERE? I USED THE RULE OF FIVE!

NOW IT'S YOUR TURN

Exercise: Transform Industry Commentary into Thought Leadership

Use the following questions as a guide to get the ball rolling:

- What do you think the next big thing will be?
- What drives you crazy?
- What thoughts about your industry keep you up at night?
- What do you wish you would have done differently while getting started in your field?
- How can you use your AND to focus your ideas in a slightly different direction?
- What do you wish people understood about your industry?
- Are there any myths about your industry that need to be set straight?
- What is a unique fact you can share in television interviews and speeches?

Learning to channel your thoughts and ideas into useful information for other people is the first crucial step in establishing credibility for your personal brand. I started small by writing blog posts and posting articles on my own LinkedIn page. I wrote about some of my favorite topics, like time management and follow-up. As those posts started to gain a bit of traction, I started to post more often. Eventually, because I had written a variety of pieces that people were reading and commenting on, I was able to stretch myself further. I started to reach out to websites like *Forbes* and *Fortune*, and now my content is regularly featured on those platforms. Remember, you are playing the long game here. Coming up with ideas for content is like working a new muscle—it can be a bit painful at first, but if you keep at it, you'll soon be surprised by how much you know and how quickly you can become a voice of your industry.

PRO TIP: YOU HAVE TO BE YOURSELF

Thought leadership is not about formulating an idea because it's what you THINK people want to hear or read about. Write about what YOU think matters.

THOUGHT LEADERSHIP IN ACTION: SPEAKING ENGAGEMENTS

Since establishing myself as a thought leader, I've been asked to share my ideas and opinions about real estate all over the world.

In just the past few months, I've been paid to speak in Monte Carlo, Abu Dhabi, and Australia (I'm racking up a lot of miles). I love speaking to interested audiences and meeting real estate brokers from other countries. People are always warm, welcoming, and engaged, and I get excited before every speech.

This is a far cry from how I felt at my first speaking engagement, which was terrifying. I remember my hands were sweating as I sat in the cab headed uptown to the venue. I was tapping my feet out of nervousness. *What if these people hate me?* I kept running through my speech in my head, hoping my audience would be receptive. I walked into the auditorium trying to shake off my fear. I took a deep breath as I was being introduced. "Good morning, seventh graders! Today we have a very special guest who is here to speak to you about success. Let's give a warm welcome to real estate broker Ryan SurHen." After mispronouncing my name, the principal glanced at her notes and gave me a look that said, *Good luck, buddy. These kids would be much happier if you were a basketball player.* I think two kids clapped, and I bet it was because they got to miss class. The next thirty minutes were a blur. My speech was awkward, my jokes fell flat, and I'm not sure my tips were helpful at all. No one threw anything at me, so I guess they didn't hate me? I was embarrassed, though. The seventh grade deserved better than my admittedly canned speech on success. I made a promise to myself that I would book another speaking engagement and that I'd be more prepared with a better speech. Now I've given more speeches than I can count, and after some trial and error, I finally cracked the code to crafting a speech that will keep people engaged.

Elements of an Engaging Speech

Provide a unique point of view. I had NOTHING new to add to the cliché "success" speech those poor middle schoolers sat through. Make sure your topic has an interesting angle. Had I gone for something like "why success doesn't matter" or "everything you've learned about success is wrong," it would have been a more engaging speech.

Keep up to date. While you need to know your topic like the back of your hand, you also need to know about any developments or changes in your field that could impact your speech. A new development in electric car technology doesn't mean your speech about "how to sell electric cars" doesn't work. You can talk about the new development and how it impacts your topic.

Authenticity, again. Let your own personality shine through. Do not stand there in front of an audience trying to be Mr. or Ms. Professional Speaker who talks like a robot. People want advice from people they like and can relate to. So, just loosen up a bit, all right?

Read the room *before you get in the room*. It is crucial that you know exactly who you are speaking to; otherwise you will end up standing up on a stage rambling while the audience naps right in front of you. How you speak to a group of seasoned bankers is going to be very different from how you handle talking to a group of new college graduates. Whenever I book a speech, I make sure we have a conversation about expectations with my contact at the organization. I want to know exactly WHO I'm talking to, the general topic they're looking for, and if there are any very specific topics they want me to address. (The answer is usually "Yes, thank you for asking and being open to talking about that." Bonus points!) Adding a few tailored points based on what the client wants is a great way to repurpose a speech to keep it fresh, but without starting from scratch.

Debrief yourself. I have learned something at every speech I've given. After I've given the speech, I always make notes about what got laughs, what topics seemed to go over well, and any great questions I was asked that I should be addressing in the speech. I keep track of the organization and the topic on a spreadsheet, which is helpful for planning future talks. If I'm speaking to a group of new real estate brokers and they LOVE my 1,000-minute rule, I'll note that. If that same group looks at me with blank stares if I tell a funny story about the time a client gave me a pig as a gift, I'll consider skipping it in the future.

Practice, Practice, and Practice Again

The two words we should all eliminate from our vocabularies are *wing* and *it*. There is no winging it when it comes to speeches. Do not get up on stage and think you know your topic so well you can just "be yourself and talk." Nor should you get up on stage and recite a speech you have memorized without trying it out. You must practice in front of your phone, a mirror, your neighbor, your dog, anyone who is willing to listen. It is crucial that you TIME yourself when you practice, because thirty minutes on a stage can feel like THREE WEEKS if you haven't planned a long enough speech. Everyone needs to prepare in a way that makes them comfortable and confident, but I find that creating a list of bullet points is best for me. I can memorize the main points and then talk more freely about each topic so I don't sound too rehearsed or stiff. Below is an example of how I prepare for a speech:

> ORGANIZATION: Fictional real estate company
> TOPIC: How to grow your personal brand
> TIME: 30 minutes

TOPIC #1: A brand is the foundation you need for a successful business.
- Story about my house flooding.
- Realization that the brand needed to be my number one focus as I built my new company.

TOPIC #2: If you aren't in control of your brand, who is?
- Story about my failed attempt to create a brand (tell purple story).
- The importance of finding your core identity.

TOPIC #3: Shout it from the mountaintop.
- How to build credibility.
- How to form partnerships and collaborations.

Wrap up: Branding is the number one most important thing today in this new world of work. Ryan, be encouraging and positive!

That might look simple, but I have rehearsed every concept on that list countless times. Prepping like this makes me feel in control but leaves me room to improvise just a bit. It also removes the stress of memorizing a speech word for word.

PRO TIP: I'M STILL OBSESSED WITH IMPROV

I have brought up improv in both of my books, and I'm bringing it up again now. I still believe there is no better way to get comfortable thinking on your feet and talking to other people than improv. Talking in front of large groups of people can be scary, but it can also be fun. To plant yourself firmly on the fun side of speaking, sign up for improv. I promise the skills you learn will be very useful as you build your brand. And yes, I still make everyone on my team take improv lessons.

There were many years between that awkward speech (sorry, seventh graders) and the one I delivered recently at a major conference in the Middle East. I would never have ended up on that stage in Abu Dhabi if I hadn't built the speaking part of my business from the ground up. In the beginning I would speak to anyone who was willing to listen to me. I emailed any local organization I could think of who might want a speaker (you'd be surprised how many people want speakers). Career day at a high school? ME, PLEASE (although tough audience, really tough). Alumni day? SIGN ME UP. Local business groups, professional organizations, career fairs . . . I did all of it. Each time I spoke, I learned how to refine my speeches to make them stronger and more impactful. I got practice talking in front of a crowd (it's definitely different from acting, where someone else has written the lines), and I made a few connections at every talk I gave. I met young people who I thought would make killer agents someday, parents who needed to upgrade to bigger homes, and local business leaders who helped connect me to other speaking opportunities. I posted about every talk I did, which cemented my position as a thought leader and resulted in being asked to give more speeches. The circle just kept growing. This took time, it took work, but every ounce of energy I devoted to this was worth it. Speaking has taken me a long way since standing in that middle school auditorium. Just check out the post of me sand surfing in Abu Dhabi to see how.

BE AN AWARD WINNER

You've heard the quote before: "Eighty percent of success is showing up." My version of that quote is "Eighty percent of winning awards is finding awards to win." Winning "salesman of the year" or being listed in a "forty people under forty" article is a great thing to have in your bio, and it equals an instant boost in your credibility. Trade publications, local business groups, and communities often have awards, and guess what? You can nominate yourself! If you are thinking, *What's the point of nominating myself? That doesn't count!*, understand that while you might be nominating yourself, it's your credentials and achievements that result in THE WIN. And chances are a good number of your competitors went ahead and nominated themselves too. So just do it, and may the best person win. To get a small but helpful extra edge, find out who won the award previously. Do some research on this person to get an understanding of what kinds of skills and achievements merit the award. This will help you prepare a shining entry that will give you the best chances of winning.

COVERAGE: YOUR BRAND OUT IN THE WORLD

In February 2021, shortly after I started SERHANT., I made a point to stop at the newsstand on the way to the office. I was feeling a night-before-Christmas, last-day-of-school level of excitement. There it was: a stack of the latest issue of *New York Magazine* with a big feature on me. *Wow, it's actually real! New York Magazine* is an internationally known publication that covers all things New York, from the best new restaurants and must-see plays to interviews with people who dress cool to features on New Yorkers who are making an impact on the city. In their fifty-five-year history, they had never done a feature on a real estate brokerage, yet inside was a detailed article about me and the founding of SERHANT.

Holding that magazine in my hand was a crazy moment. I knew I had worked hard to become truly successful, and life had changed for the better as a result. I didn't have to buy any more clearance rack suits! I lived in a real house with multiple bathrooms with my family instead of strangers. I went on vacations, and I was the CEO of my own company. But holding that magazine in my hand might as well have been a trophy that said CONGRATULATIONS, RYAN SERHANT. YOU MADE IT! I had been covered in the press before, and I had done many interviews, but this magazine feature mattered so much because it was the best piece of earned media I had gotten. This wasn't someone asking me my opinion on a topic for an article they were writing; my business was the focus. It wasn't an advertisement that I paid for, controlling the exact message I wanted to share, either. It was the result of the work I put into building my brand and bulking up my credibility. I *earned the right* to warrant media coverage at this level. I must have stood at the newsstand staring at the cover of this magazine for a long time, because a voice snapped me out of my joy-induced trance: "Hey, buddy, you gonna buy something or what?" I bought every copy.

It took over ten years to earn the right to be featured in that magazine. Just like speaking, I started out small. Very small. The first paper to ever run coverage of me was a local newspaper in Steamboat Springs, Colorado. It was a short article that talked about my new real estate career in New York. I got this

feature because my parents lived there, and I had lived there during the summer when I was in college, and the paper liked the idea of a story about "a local kid trying to make it in the big city." It was my first stepping-stone on what would become a very long path leading to other coverage and eventually to *New York Magazine*.

At first, the idea of getting press for myself sounded crazy. *Who am I to think someone should write about ME?* Getting press for yourself isn't about waiting around for someone to discover you. It isn't about waiting for YOU to be the best or have a massive achievement under your belt (although things like that to shout about help). Instead, you need to take your best assets and achievements and package them. You need to get out there and ask for it until that first reporter says yes, giving you the Big Unlock. That very first piece of media unlocks a big, heavy door, and it's the first important step to getting bigger coverage. To get your Big Unlock, you need the following tools:

1. **The Press Kit.** Everything about your press kit needs to be polished and credible. It should contain your bio and company profile. Be sure to include awards, thought leadership creds, speaking you've done, what key topics you focus on, and substantive rankings like *I was the number one golf instructor at the Really Good Golf Club three years in a row.* The goal is to show-case yourself as the person journalists NEED to talk to about topics relating to X.

2. **The Media List.** Your media list is an up-to-date document (*up-to-date* being a very key phrase here) that includes the contact information for reporters who

cover topics that pertain to your area of expertise. Start your media list by noting all the print newspapers, local and popular bloggers, websites, influencers, business journals, and local news and television stations. Often you will find an about page, and this will list different writers and the topics they cover. Follow these people on social media. Comment when they post something. Show how useful and knowledgeable you are. Following them is also a way to learn what their interests are and what they've already covered. Up-to-date is important because the idea is you're developing relationships with these people. When a contact changes, you need to know so you can continue pitching to the right people. It can be challenging to keep this up, so this is a good time to consider paying for extra help. You can hire a local PR professional who will have all the contacts you could need, or you can subscribe to a service like pressrush.com, which is a media list database.

3. **The Pitch.** You've created a top-notch press kit and have familiarized yourself with the right media outlets and the correct contacts. Now you go in with your pitch. You'll want to write a short but friendly email explaining who you are and offer a few stories about different topics (this is where you lean on all those thought leadership ideas). Offer data or specific information that shows how this story is relevant NOW. Never, ever mass email these. They should be individualized for each person, and because you're following them on social and reading their work *you can compliment them on a story of theirs that you found helpful.*

PRO TIP: YOUR NEWSLETTER ISN'T FOR EVERYONE

Do not send media contacts your newsletter. Get in touch only to pitch a specific story or to offer them help by providing useful information.

NOW IT'S YOUR TURN

Exercise: Use the Essential Elements to Craft a Good Pitch Letter

Reference an article they wrote: I loved your story about the new technology of running shoes. I have shared your insightful article with many of my clients.

Share credentials: I am a certified fitness instructor and have been listed as the number one trainer for the third year in a row in the *Northern New Jersey Times*. I am an elite runner who has finished fifteen marathons in different parts of the country, and my specialty is preparing runners of all skill levels for their first marathon. I recently trained a seventy-seven-year-old woman who has always wanted to run a marathon. She exceeded her expected time and is planning to run again next year.

Offer help: As an expert in long-distance running, I have years of experience helping new runners face the immense challenge that is running a marathon. I've developed a training program and nutrition plan that have helped countless runners make it across the finish line. More people than ever are running marathons, with over a million people participating in a marathon each year. According to Yale Medicine, 50 percent of runners are injured every year. I see you write extensively about fitness and wellness, and I have proven techniques for preventing such injuries that anyone can easily do.

Stop right there. Do not attach anything (that's just asking to end up in the spam folder). This is all you need to do. Just keep in mind that once you've offered help to a media outlet you must be prepared to jump into action. Media turnaround can be lightning fast. If a reporter calls me and says, "Ryan! I need you to speak about increasing interest rates on a segment that's airing at noon today," the only answer is YES. I'm on my way. It wouldn't matter if my hair looked terrible or I had spilled half of my protein shake on my shirt. I'd get a comb to fix my hair and get a new shirt faster than I could open the Uber app to take me to a studio. Once you show you're a reliable source, you're more likely to become a go-to person for that editor or producer.

PRO TIP: A PUBLICIST IS THE BEST FIRST HIRE

One of the first people I ever hired when I started selling real estate was a publicist. Since then, I have always had a publicist on staff or on retainer. It is an investment, but an excellent one. While you CAN have success in doing this yourself, being pitched to media outlets by a professional publicist is like being introduced with a stamp of approval that says, *This person is media-worthy.*

YOU'RE OUT THERE! KEEP PRACTICING!

I've already mentioned that I've adjusted how I talk on television thanks to watching myself look ridiculous in front of millions of people. I've also worked hard to perfect how I speak to journalists. It's important to come off as confident, informed, and trustworthy. Saying *um* every two seconds practically shouts I'M NEW AT THIS. I still practice. Before every interview, TV appearance, or speech, I review notes I've created the night before. I want to make sure my commentary is fresh and helpful. I will never stop practicing because I want to get better and be polished enough to appeal to top outlets like the *New York Times*, the *Washington Post*, the *Wall Street Journal*, nightly news programs, morning programs, and talk shows. And guess what? The people who are sought-out thought leaders work very hard to make sure they're on their best game.

Iman Gadzhi, founder of IAG Media, wanted to start taking his YouTube game more seriously: "I was putting out a lot of content, so I thought I should try to reach more people. I thought I had a good message, but my delivery was totally off. I'm the kind of guy who would hit record and just start talking for thirty minutes, but people didn't like that. I started to really refine my cadence and delivery."

Tom Bilyeu has made a deliberate decision to become a top-notch commentator: "I think I've done almost nine hundred interviews by now. They drive revenue and awareness, and the more I do the better I get. It's about putting in reps and wanting to be the best. The Best of the best. I'm not there yet, so I'm going to keep pushing my skill set." The more you practice, the better you'll get, and the brighter your brand will shine under the spotlight.

COMMUNITY: EVEN BETTER THAN BIG NUMBERS

All of these tactics are meant to increase your audience, but it's important to understand that having an audience is just the beginning. To increase brand awareness and promote loyalty, you must turn your audience into a community. Nadya Okamoto, cofounder of August, a lifestyle brand working to reimagine periods and founder of PERIOD, an organization fighting to end period poverty and stigma, has kept her community front and center while building her personal brand. "The brand-building process was very community oriented. Everything we did, from the language we used, to the choosing of colors, to choosing the name was something we did in partnership as a team. But we also had a growing community that we called our inner circle that we host on the app Geneva (think: Slack for Gen Z). We didn't do anything without running it by the community and getting ideas and feedback. We're schooled and humbled every single day on assumptions we made around what resonates with our community." Okamoto's approach to building her brand collaboratively is the exact opposite of what brand building used to be—people in a boardroom with a whiteboard coming up with a product to put out into the world.

Okamoto chooses to include her community in product development as well. "When we were figuring out what the final product was going to be for our tampons and pads, we thought, *Let's get samples; let's try them out as a team and pick our favorite.*" While her approach is unique, fostering a community has brought her much closer to her core audience: "There's a lot of value to having a close-knit community. I feel very strongly that your social media audience is not a community; it's an audience. Our community is internal, and it's closed off; it's more intimate. There's a big difference between audience and community. An audience can be a lot of fans, but it can also be made of people who are skeptical or haters. The way I try to differentiate in my mind is that if there's an audience, I'm the one with the microphone. Community is where my role as a brand is not to have a microphone but to be the event planner, hosting an open table where everybody else is talking and discussing. I'm really there to hold the space."

At SERHANT., we think about the differences between audience and community like this:

> **Audience = people you speak TO**
> **Community = people you speak WITH**

We have a thriving community at SERHANT., and we've created a few different ways for people to interact with us. Our education arm creates online classes on topics that help real estate brokers sharpen their skills. I share my own tips and tricks, and we also bring in experts to share their knowledge on topics like PR and creating ads for social media. We've done classes on sales techniques, branding, and closing and negotiation tactics. People who sign up for our classes get access to the SERHANT. Connect Referral Network. This connects agents from different parts of the country for lead referrals. For example, if a SERHANT. agent on Long Island has a lead for a buyer in Boston, they can use SERHANT. Connect to refer that lead to another trusted agent. We also created the Pro Network Community. This is a paid program that offers training, coaching, and mentorship and attracts agents who are looking to take their career to the next level. These agents are invited to weekly Q&As with me and can connect on our Facebook group. Our Mastermind Dinners have also become popular, and we hold them a few times a year in different parts of the country. These dinners have a higher ticket price, but we limit them to a small number of agents, so everyone gets attention. I host a fun sit-down dinner to kick things off. We've held them in Las Vegas and Chicago and once in my $250 million listing with the insane view at Central Park Tower. These multi-day events include my keynote speech, talks from experts in different areas, breakout groups, and a lot of fun socializing. For one of our Masterminds in Manhattan, I invited anyone who wanted to join me for a workout on the roof of our building. Nothing bonds and connects people like sweat.

While many of these events are money-making ventures for us (I am running a business, after all!), there is a lot of goodwill that comes out of these communities. Agents share knowledge, swap stories about tricky deals, talk about listings they're excited about, and discuss what's going on in their own markets. The communities we've created support the idea that the SERHANT. brand is more than a company that sells real estate. We are here to share everything we've learned, because as any real estate agent knows, there is no instruction booklet. We are invested in the success of agents everywhere.

GLEE: THE WAY TO BUILD HAPPY AND USEFUL COMMUNITIES

So, how do you turn lurkers who are just hanging around and not engaging with your brand into a community? First and foremost, a community is about engagement *and* belonging. That feeling of belonging to something special is the result of participating in ritualized onboarding. *Don't freak out.* This ritualization does not involve chanting in a circle under a full moon. It's simply any process that each new member experiences. It could be a welcome letter, new member introductions, new member spotlights that showcase their profiles, an invitation to a new member webinar, onboarding or orientation videos, or anything you want to do that says, *Hey, we're glad you're here!* Extra resources that are only available to community members make people feel included. You could offer member Q&As, early access to events, or newsletters. Some communities are built around NFTs, and token holders are privy to early access for concert tickets or reservations at a members-only restaurant.

Communities have the added advantage of developing an interest in one another's success, which is a big difference from being in an audience, where members usually stand alone. Happy communities build trust and loyalty, but they also act as a reinforcement of your brand message. You just need to listen to what your community tells you they want! You also want to foster your community so that it grows with your members. All of the gathering, listening, engaging, and evolving become the real process for scaling both your community and your brand. To build a thriving community, use GLEE:

> **Gather:** Gather your brand followers in a space where they can connect with each other and hear directly from you.
> **Listen:** Listen to their feedback! How is your brand being perceived, and is it aligned with your brand vision?
> **Engage:** Engage by posing questions, starting conversations, and sharing thoughts and ideas. The idea is to create an environment where community members feel like they belong. I like to reply to select comments. I want to encourage people to leave comments, and they are more likely to if they know I interact with my community. No matter how busy my schedule gets, I want the SERHANT. community to know that I'm there and willing to engage!
> **Evolve:** As your brand evolves, your community should evolve with you. There should be a sense of "everyone being in it together."

You can get as creative as you want with the benefits you offer community members, and whatever you decide to offer benefits you too. Fostering a strong community *strategically* is an easy way to repeatedly transform customers into audience members who will be brand advocates for life.

A GUIDE FOR RESPONDING TO COMMENTS

You can't respond to every comment, so you need to be selective about who you choose to interact with.

YES! Respond to:

Insightful questions: Good questions are likely something other people will find interesting, or maybe they're even wondering the exact same thing. I find insightful questions to be great conversation starters.

Well-worded constructive feedback: I am always looking to improve! I'll happily reply to useful feedback. I want to know if I'm being annoying or doing something wrong.

Kind thoughts and sentiments: Who doesn't like to hear something nice? Have manners—say thank you!

Funny comments: I like funny people. If you make me laugh, I'll let you know.

NO! Do NOT respond to:

Super-negative comments: There's no point, as they typically warrant only a negative response, and why would you want to encourage that?

Bad/lazy questions: If someone asks, "What's the price of this listing?" on a post where the price is listed RIGHT THERE, I'm not going to reply (and I'm judging you in my mind).

Favors: TONS of people send messages and leave comments where they're just asking for favors, like, "Ryan, can you help me find a buyer for my listing?" As much as I'd like to help everyone, I just don't have a hundred hours in my day.

I know this feels like a lot, and it is. But trust me that focusing on credibility, coverage, and community makes getting up that mountaintop so you can start SHOUTING much easier and more sustainable. Think of those three components as your team of sherpas, standing by your side as you begin the trek up your very own Mount Everest. Do you know what happens to people who climb Everest without the proper training, tools, and know-how? They. Do. Not. Survive. You are not going to be left in the cold on the side of the mountain gasping for air, admitting defeat before you're anywhere near the top. You're about to embark on a long and hard journey, but you're going about it the right way. As soon as you hit a tough spot and it feels like *you can't keep shouting about your brand for even one more second*, that credibility you honed will lead to coverage on a local TV show, and TA-DA . . . you will get the very boost you need to keep going. In those moments when you're not sure what's next—Do I put a foot here? Or will I plunge to my death if I do that, and all of this will be for nothing? Remember that you're not alone and figuring everything out for yourself; there's a community behind you, cheering you on and providing guidance when you need it most. I and many of the people I've interviewed in this book might be on top of the mountain right now. Sure, the view is great up here, but the truth is the work doesn't just end once you're at the top. A storm can knock you down, you can lose your grip and fall a bit, but that's okay. You don't make it up this high without learning many valuable lessons along the way, and these lessons will serve you forever. Take a minute to gather your strength, and know I'll be waiting for you, hand outstretched, when you get to the top.

The first chapter of Phase Three: Shout It from the Mountaintop has prepared you for your brand's first big foray into the world. You've gotten your brand ready for this moment by accomplishing all of the following (it was a lot, I know!):

Upping your credibility game ✔
Transforming thoughts into thought leadership by:
    Leaning on your AND ✔
    Being an outlier ✔
    Daring to predict ✔
    The unique fact technique ✔
    The rule of five ✔
Studying the elements of an engaging speech ✔
Preparing for press coverage by working on your:
    Press kit ✔
    Media list ✔
    Pitch letter ✔
Using GLEE: Gather, listen, engage, evolve to build communities ✔
Examining which comments should and should not receive responses ✔

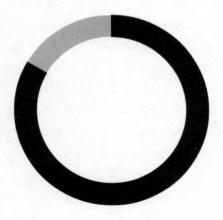

NOW IT'S SYDNEY'S TURN

CREDIBILITY AND COVERAGE

1. **What drives you crazy?**

   Any influencer who claims to have the universal "secret sauce" for accomplishing XYZ goal—e.g., "If you start your morning THIS WAY, you'll be the most productive person on the planet!" or "If you do THESE THREE EXERCISES, you'll have toned arms in five days!"

2. **What thoughts about your industry keep you up at night?**

   That fitness professionals take anecdotal evidence and promote it at scale. What works for you doesn't work for everyone, and that's not as sexy as a quick fix, but it deserves WAY more recognition.

3. **What do you wish you would have done differently while getting started in your field?**

   I'm grateful that I had the experiences I did when I got started; otherwise, I don't think I'd see the flaws in our industry as clearly as I do now. What I'd love to influence is how other people kick-start their own fitness journey—I'd love for more of us to start by becoming super self-aware and less reliant on what social media tells us is "healthy" or the best approach.

4. **How can you use your AND to focus your ideas in a slightly different direction?**

   My AND is that I'm a busy, successful professional. My AND comes into play when I want to demonstrate to my clients that no matter what, there IS a way that you can integrate a wellness routine into even your busiest, most stressful day.

5. **What do you wish people understood about your industry?**

   Often, what we *actually* do to accomplish our goals isn't what SELLS. Start caring less about the headlines and more about what makes YOU feel good.

6. **Are there any myths about your industry that need to be set straight?**

   This list would go on forever, but in short . . . YES.

THOUGHTS FROM SYDNEY

Finding press contacts to pitch can feel intimidating, but the best tip I've received from fellow SERHANT'er Kyle Scott was to leverage resources writers use when *they need* your help, like *Help a Reporter Out*. If there's a topic posted for an article I feel I can contribute value to, and it aligns with my brand, then I pitch it!

COMMUNITY

Developing a strong, engaged community takes a lot of time and a lot of trust, but the route that I've decided to start with is:

1. Nurturing an AUDIENCE on social media through content on Instagram and TikTok (sharing helpful, relevant content, replying to comments, replying to DMs, engaging with other creators, etc.).
2. Teeing up the conversion from AUDIENCE > COMMUNITY by developing a newsletter and nurturing the subscriber audience.

In the future, I see the Self by Syd community growing through in-person workouts, events, and meet and greets, and through virtual programming options.

CHAPTER 13

Partnerships: The Art of a Good Hookup

Forging partnerships is one of the best things you can do for your personal brand. Partnerships are a way to monetize, expand your reach, and enhance your reputation even further. Searching for the best kind of partnership can feel a bit like dating. You won't get the best results if you're just hanging out at a nightclub looking for the shiniest and most attractive option. Trust me when I say that the worst thing you can do is desperately jump into bed with the first brand who so much as looks your way!

To get serious about forging a lasting partnership, you need to get clear on what you're looking for; otherwise, you run the risk of connecting with a brand that might seem appealing but in the end doesn't make sense for you AT ALL. It's like if Barbie broke up with Ken to start a partnership with a Spider-Man action figure. Not that there's anything wrong with this per se, it's just not a mutually beneficial partnership. Sure, Barbie and Spider-Man both bring some interesting abilities to the table. Barbie's strengths include good style, an eye for design (not just anyone can pull off a mansion with no facade), the ability to wear stilettos 24/7, spreading cheer, and a résumé that includes every job path on earth, from doctor to professional surfer. Spider-Man is part of the Marvel Universe version of New York City, which is rife with crime and villains like the Green Goblin, who flies around the city on his glider causing havoc with his state-of-the-art firepower, and Electro, who shoots lightning from his fingertips. Spider-Man's strengths are saving humans from peril, climbing buildings, and huffing around town as his alter ego taking photographs for the *Daily Bugle*. Spider-Man might be tempted to escape to Barbie's super-pink universe that's full of convertibles and sunshine, but he *belongs* in the Marvel hellscape of New York City because fighting crime is his purpose. Not to mention his spiderwebs would be rendered useless with Barbie, because again, *her house doesn't have walls*. They both have their own unique strengths, but one doesn't help out the other. To decide whether a partnership is on brand for you, you need to know that your values won't be compromised, that the strengths you bring to the table will be highlighted, and that you'll be connecting to the right audience.

DOES THIS PARTNERSHIP COMPROMISE YOUR VALUES?

Partnerships are undeniably a great way to monetize your personal brand and expand your audience. However, neither of those things is worth it if it comes at the expense of undermining your values, sending your credibility into the toilet. There is no amount of money and no level of growth that's worth throwing your integrity out the window, where it will be stomped on relentlessly, leaving behind a sad pile of ashes. FaZe Clan, the e-gaming platform, has an envy-inducing list of partnerships, and they've been deliberate about keeping their values in check. Sebastian Diamond a.k.a. FaZe CBass says, "It's critically important that we don't do anything that makes it seem like we've lost that cool factor. If people who follow our brand are consuming and paying attention to what another brand is doing, I know we can go there." FaZe Clan's partnerships include Porsche, Nissan, the artist Takashi Murakami, Xbox 360, McDonald's, DoorDash, Totino's, Xfinity, and a FaZe Clan–branded Nike shoe that was designed with and is worn by LeBron James *on the court*. "If there's a brand that has nothing to do with video games and never will, we won't work with them. Twelve years ago, Porsche would never have entered the space because gamers weren't cool and weren't the type of people who buy Porsches. Now that's not true. Now it makes sense for a brand like Porsche to go where we go next, because gamers are actually the ones making the money and buying cars like that." Another reason FaZe Clan is open to partnerships is because these relationships help make one of their key values a possibility, which is to not take money away from the players: "We don't actually make that much off of prize money. The players do, and that's an important model that has kept eSports alive, because these guys are spending literally their entire day practicing to compete in these events. And if they weren't able to make the prize money from doing so, it wouldn't be worth it for them to do it. We take enough to cover the cost of running the team, but the large majority and sometimes all of it goes back to the players. So, partnerships are one of the primary ways for us to earn income. Partnerships are ultimately what keeps the business alive."

Author Mark Manson believes understanding your values from the beginning and knowing *why people love you* plays a crucial role in deciding what you will and won't do: "It's understanding the values you stand for, or the values you represent, then not compromising those. Any brand that becomes successful is going to get a lot of opportunity to compromise those values to make a quick buck. So, you have to really know what you stand for, and you need to know why people love you in the first place. For me, it comes back to honesty, no bullshit, humor, being candid, but also a big part of my brand is that I am critical of the conventional self-help industry. I don't put on big seminars because I don't think they're that useful. I don't go on all the morning talk shows (oh, they don't really want me because I have the word *fuck* in my book). There's a lot of stuff around media and television that I pass up because I'm like, "Yeah, it's not authentic. It's not a reflection of my brand or what people love me for." If you start spreading something way too thin, it starts losing its significance for other people."

As you're building your brand, think carefully about how your values will play a role in exploring partnerships, because in the end, shouting about your brand from the mountaintop is as much about what you decide *not to do* as what you decide *to* do.

DOES THE PARTNERSHIP HIGHLIGHT THE STRENGTHS OF YOUR BRAND?

A partnership that highlights your brand's strengths can lead to new ideas and products. Rebecca Minkoff, known for her downtown, rock 'n' roll aesthetic, forged a partnership with the investment banking firm Morgan Stanley. "We're always pitching creative ideas to bigger brands, but this one was inbound. Morgan Stanley was looking for a designer to partner with to co-ideate a banker bag for women. There's a stigma on Wall Street about these men's sports bags that they use to play pickleball. Because what is the women's version of that? So, we said, 'Let's not just do a bag. Let's have you headline and be the premiere sponsor of our show, since that's how you're going to get the most media.'" The partnership worked, and each brand got positive media attention. "For them it was an insane amount of engagement, mentions, and positioning." The bags were also a huge success, which was another win for Minkoff. "Within Stanley Morgan, they were fighting over the bags. They ordered three hundred and came back and ordered one thousand." The partnership also created goodwill for Morgan Stanley, and Minkoff's designs were in the hands of a potentially new audience. "The women were saying, 'Yes, we want this symbol and we're excited about it.'" Both brands brought their own strengths to the table, and sharing their resources resulted in wins for both sides.

However, while I obviously think SERHANT. is one of the best brands ever (yes, I know I'm biased), it doesn't mean everyone should collaborate with me. If I called up Nadya Okamoto, cofounder of August, and said, *Hey! Let's do a collaboration! It will be amazing!*, it shouldn't surprise me if her response was, "Ryan, my brand is about fighting period poverty and stigma, which has NOTHING at all to do with luxury real estate. So, that's a pass from me and good luck to you!" Collaborations must benefit both sides to have a big impact.

WILL THE PARTNERSHIP MAKE YOUR AUDIENCE HAPPY?

Justina Blakeney, founder of Jungalow, has a maximalist style that has landed her on the cover of *Architectural Digest*, and she's been featured in *Harper's Bazaar*; *O, the Oprah Magazine*; *Good Housekeeping*; *House Beautiful*; and *Essence*. Jungalow, which started as a blog and went on to become a huge presence on Pinterest, started a collaboration with Target in 2021. Blakeney has learned that the more excited she gets about a partnership, the more likely it is that her audience will be excited too: "I am at a place in my life and in my career where I don't say yes unless it's a hell yes. It's very instinctive. If something comes down the pipeline and I'm thinking *Oh, I can't wait to talk about this*, it's a sign that it's a hell yes. I strongly believe that the integrity of the brand is about keeping everything we do very exciting to me. If it doesn't excite me, if it doesn't light me up, if it doesn't give me that hell yes feeling, I know it's not going to do that for my audience either. That's my barometer."

Blakeney's collection with Target, called Opalhouse by Jungalow, now features three hundred different products, including bedding, bath, home decor, furniture, and wallpaper. "I'm actually pleased with how much creative control I have. I'm pretty specific about what I design and how I want things to be, and it's been a really great process." As appealing as a collaboration might be to you, thinking about how your core audience will respond to it is an important part of maintaining the flavor and personality of your brand. A potential partner's audience needs to align with your audience. There needs to be crossover in the interests and desires of your partner's audience to get meaningful results for your brand.

YOU NEVER KNOW WHERE A PARTNERSHIP WILL TAKE YOU

One of my first big partnerships was with Chase Bank. They approached me shortly after my first book, *Sell It Like Serhant*, came out. They were looking to promote their mortgage services, and they sent me around the country to speak to large groups of agents. Not only was I getting attention for my brand, but the partnership brought me a few business surprises. A few years (YEARS!) after I had done a talk for Chase in Las Vegas, I got a call from a broker who had attended the event.

> Ryan:
>
> You don't know me, but I was at your talk in Las Vegas! It was great, and now I have some business to send your way. I have a client here in Nevada who is interested in one of your properties in Manhattan. His budget is between 15 and 20 million. I might have said you were one of my closest friends SO of course I could get him in to see this amazing apartment. Let's talk and make a sale!
>
> Thanks, Mr. Nevada

We closed on an apartment for Mr. Nevada's client on West Twenty-First Street for about $15 million . . . years after the speech!

THE CHICKEN AND EGG PROBLEM

You may be in the early stages of building your brand, and the closest thing you have to a partnership with Target is the fact that you shop there. I know there is a long way to go from setting up your social media accounts and creating a content calendar to thinking, *Huh, I wonder if this lucrative partnership with company X and their audience of millions will be mutually beneficial for me?* Enter the chicken and egg problem, which is The Worst. Rebecca Minkoff describes it perfectly: "Until you get to a certain point, no one wants to hear from you, see you, or pay for your stuff, but you need exposure to get to that point." How do you get someone to care AT ALL about what you have to say when you're just a regular person with a personal brand that's just getting off the ground?

GET YOUR OWN EGGS

Until you've reached a level where "people want to hear from you," sometimes you have no choice other than to get your own eggs. You need to get creative and find a way to provide something that people will want and that has the potential to grow. When Alison Roman no longer had her column at a major newspaper, she realized it was time to focus on creating a newsletter to get her recipes and ideas in front of more eyes. "The biggest shift came when I started doing the newsletter. It has evolved a lot since I started it, and I don't think I had anticipated it growing as much as it has grown." Roman's newsletter is a subscription-based service that arrives weekly with a video called "Home Movies" that are candid videos of her making a dish. "The newsletter became more focused, and the brand became more me and not just my recipes. Now I'm a full-fledged person, rather than just a byline on a recipe document." Roman's newsletter has continued to grow, and her YouTube channel has half a million subscribers. Her newsletter has shown her audience what she has to offer: great recipes with a no-nonsense attitude and an air of familiarity (she spills on her shirt sometimes, and she's been known to use less-than-perfect equipment, like a warped cutting board) that makes you excited to see what she's cooking.

PRO TIP: RIDE ON COATTAILS, SHARE YOUR COATTAILS

When you are in the earlier stages of brand building, sometimes the best way to create awareness for yourself is to gently, kindly, ask to collaborate with someone whose brand meshes with yours. Maybe you could do a video together, a live chat, or just get them to follow you. As your brand grows, don't forget how hard it is to deal with the chicken and egg problem. Offer a ride on your coattails to help a new brand you like.

Ryan Holiday, author and media strategist, started dealing with his egg problem before it became an issue: "In 2008 or 2009,

I knew I wanted to get serious about being a writer, and I had gotten this advice that I should start an email list. I thought, "Why would anyone subscribe to the email list of a person they had never heard of? Why would anyone just follow Ryan Holiday when he's never done anything or published anything?" There's this chicken and egg thing with personal brands where you want people to follow your brand, but why would they do that? I decided I would start an email list of book recommendations. Once a month I would send out a list of book recommendations, and I started out with about ten people. Now it's in the hundreds of thousands."

Holiday was able to use this list as proof that his personal brand had reach when he got ready to sell his first book to publishers: "By acting as a conduit or broker, you develop trust and prove your taste. That list was the one thing I had (other than my idea for the book) when I went into publishers so I could say, 'Hey, I'm not some random person off the street. I do have a track record of getting people to buy books.'" Holiday wasn't just proving that he could connect with an audience; he was showing that his personal brand had value. "I think what all artists and entrepreneurs do is create value for people. And originally, that value was in the form of recommending other books."

To create your own eggs so you ideally end up with chickens—and ta-da, more eggs—think about what kind of value you can bring to people as you're building an audience for your brand. Consider trying out tutorials, newsletters, recommendations, how-to videos, or Q&As. It doesn't matter if you start with five people and two of them are your parents. By finding a way to provide value and doing it consistently, you can establish yourself as that funny person who is giving great advice about life while doing amazing nail art tutorials, or the brilliant painter who does portraits of people on the street while talking about how to tap into your creativity. The key is to have a sense of urgency here. Find a way to show your value NOW. If you wait for someone to come knocking on your door because they heard you're the best skateboarder in the world and they want you to wear their brand's T-shirts, you will be waiting around FOR THE REST OF YOUR LIFE. Create your own egg, coax it to life, and see how many chickens you end up with.

Sebastian Diamond feels partnerships are important for an entire industry to survive and thrive. "I think partnerships and collaborations are the lifeblood of brand. I think what makes those partnerships very valuable is that while we view ourselves as the pinnacle of the industry, we are very much a part of that industry, and we need it to survive, thrive, and grow in order for us to do the same." He also sees FaZe Clan's success in co-branding as evidence that it can happen for any brand. "It's one step along the way. A lot of our partnerships are the first time a brand has come into our space. When we bring a partner like Porsche or Nike into our space, we're telling every other brand that you can do it too."

After several decades of running a massively successful brand, Kenneth Cole has come to see that every potential customer of his is in itself a brand, and every customer is a potential branding partner: "Today, everybody is their own brand. Everyone wakes up in the morning and curates their own brand on their Facebook page, Instagram, TikTok, Twitter, or whatever they use. Not only do they curate their own content, but they curate their own audience. My job today is to have a collaboration—to have people agree to co-brand and allow *me* to be part of their brand, how they introduce themselves to the world, and how they decide what they're going to look like. It's a critical choice people make every day, and I'm hoping people allow me to be part of it."

You don't need to have a collaboration with a major retailer or a car manufacturer to successfully partner with another brand. Each follower and every audience member equals a potential brand to collaborate with. Every connection you make is another opportunity to cocreate or be inspired by another brand, big or small. Your brand's value is your most precious possession, but you have to share it to get noticed. It starts with just one step: creating that first interesting egg that will show everyone how much you actually have to offer.

You did it. You're at the end of Phase Three, and you should be buzzing with excitement because you've accomplished so much, including:

Determining whether a partnership meshes with your
  brand values ✔
Ensuring a partnership would highlight your strengths ✔
Anticipating if a partnership is right for your audience ✔
Making a plan to solve your chicken and egg situation ✔

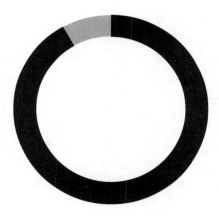

NOW IT'S SYDNEY'S TURN

PARTNERSHIPS

In my experience, there are two tiers of partnerships I pursue:

1. Tier One: small-to-medium wellness brands actively looking to partner with other fitness professionals
    a. New/intermediate wellness brands that are part of my own daily routine (think: LMNT, Celsius, MadeMeals Co., Aneva, Trooper Fitness, etc.)
    b. Other trainers in the city (think: cohosting events, co-branding marketing initiatives, etc.)
    c. Community events (think: Astoria Open Street's free workouts, etc.)
2. Tier Two: larger, established wellness brands with existing partnerships, harder pitch
    a. Corporate partnerships (think: coaching a bulk of sessions for a corporate sponsor)
    b. Becoming a Nike/Adidas/Lululemon/Vuori ambassador
    c. Becoming a race ambassador (think: Hyrox)

No matter what partnership I'm pursuing or vetting, the key for me is to make sure there's strong brand alignment and mutual benefit. My favorite partnership to date has been with a friend's business, Movement & Mindset.

Jane VanderVoort, founder of M&M, was one of the first coaches I connected with when I started personal training here in the city. She was incredibly supportive and eager to see me succeed, and she offered to mentor me through my first few months as a coach. Fast-forward to one year later, Jane was building out her roster of coaches for Movement & Mindset small-group fitness classes, and she connected with me to join the team.

Because of her eagerness to help me, share her expertise, and provide me with the resources to succeed, I knew that aligning Self by Syd with Movement & Mindset would be a strong partnership, and so far it's been amazing working with her and our joint clients!

FINAL THOUGHTS FROM SYDNEY

As a brand builder and educator, I walked into these exercises feeling like it'd be nothing more than reassuring—I have the process down; it's just a little slow to grow! But completing the exercises in *Brand It Like Serhant* did more than I could have anticipated.

At moments, the reassurance was absolutely there, but I also felt held accountable to processes I've slacked on and felt empowered with clarity I didn't even realize I needed. I feel like I've hired a whole branding agency for the price of a book. Overall, my brand feels more cohesive, intentional, and aligned with my vision for it. I am so excited to see Self by Syd grow, and I'm grateful to Ryan for sharing his infinite branding wisdom with business owners like me! You can do this!

CHAPTER 14

Get Ready to Be Transformed

Building your personal brand isn't just an important business move that everyone needs to make. Building a brand is *transformative*. SERHANT. isn't just a brand; it's like my very own bridge to success that can take me as far as I want to go. That bridge has taken me to places that I didn't think I would see, because for a long time I didn't think I belonged. I didn't have the right background or connections, or the kind of firsthand knowledge that people who grew up in New York City have. But every step I take across that bridge gets me further away from the insecure rookie broker I used to be and brings me closer to the future me who is UNSTOPPABLE.

Building a brand is long, hard work, but it can lead you to places you've wanted to go *but didn't know how to get to.* When I finally stepped off the bridge I'd spent years building, it was like I was handed my own personal golden key to the universe. My golden key has given me a whole new level of access—tables at impossible-to-get-into restaurants, invites to social events at huge Hamptons estates, travel by private jet, and invites to speak at conferences all over the world. Those things are important, but they're just one part of the picture. That golden key is a shining reminder to myself that because of my personal brand I can achieve anything. My confidence, knowledge, skills, connections, and team are there to support me no matter how high I want to reach. A few months ago, my golden key opened up an opportunity to close a huge deal in the most unexpected place imaginable.

After a big year, it was time to recharge and relax, so Emilia and I planned a long weekend at a small, ultra-luxurious Caribbean island known for insanely beautiful beaches. This island we love is a challenge to get to, so many of the exclusive visitors are dropped off by their yachts or fly in on their private jets. The hotels manage to be glamorous and idyllic at once, and they attract some of the wealthiest and most powerful people in the world. We had just finished dinner on our first night on the island. The food was amazing, the restaurant had an incredible view, and after dinner I was ready for my favorite vacation indulgence . . . ice cream. The restaurant was high end, and the dessert menu had fancy offerings like *meringue croustillante au Timut, fruit de saison,* or *Crêpes dentelles, crème légère au rhum ambré.* As good as I'm sure crunchy merengue with seasonal fruit or crepes with cream and amber rum is, my inner twelve-year-old just wants ice cream when I'm on vacation.

After asking a local to draw a map on a napkin, Emilia and I climbed into our rental car, which was essentially a go-cart, and headed off into the island night in search of my favorite vacation treat. It's like I have an internal radar that detects ice cream. I've found ice cream stores in the Maldives, and once on a Greek island that was so small I'm not even sure it has a name. After

a bumpy ride on what was *maybe* a road, I saw a small building and the beautiful sight of people standing around eating ice
cream cones. We parked our go-cart in the dirt, and I got in line.
As I was waiting for my order, I saw a man in line who I recognized. *Oh my God, is that Professor Ira Niekehle, the billionaire
inventor?! What is HE doing here eating ice cream in the middle
of nowhere?* I had never met Professor Niekehle, but I had been
involved in a long, drawn-out negotiation with his broker that
didn't go anywhere. He was trying to buy an apartment from
one of my clients, but it was complicated because technically the
apartment wasn't actually up for sale, and my client wasn't interested in moving.

A few months earlier, a broker had called and asked if I had
any listings in a very sought-after building uptown. The broker
literally said, "My clients were visiting friends there, and they love
the brand of the building." The brand personality of this building
is exclusive, expensive, and hard to get into, and living there is
like walking around with a sign on your back that says I HAVE
REACHED THE PINNACLE OF SUCCESS. I didn't have any
active listings in that building, but a client of mine had bought
an apartment there a few years earlier. LaLa Von Edison was an
heiress to a chocolate fortune. She loved her apartment. She had
settled in with her husband and three kids and was known for
throwing chic parties for the fabulously wealthy. *I wonder if I
could convince her it's time to upgrade?* I called LaLa, who I knew
would say NO if I just asked her if she wanted to sell. Instead, I
explained the situation and said, *Why don't we see what he can
afford?* She didn't say yes, but she didn't say no, which I took as
a sign that the right number might convince her.

What resulted was an epic back-and-forth game of negotiation that included staggeringly high numbers, and I still wasn't sure my client wanted to play. This didn't stop me though. The number I eventually presented to LaLa after what felt like years of negotiating was huge, but still not as huge as the number she had in her head. Since this offer was dropped in her lap, she didn't have to go through any of the trouble that usually goes into selling a house. There were no stagers coming in, and she didn't have to leave while I brought in prospective buyers. This situation was essentially the equivalent of a super-rich guy knocking on your door and offering you a pile of money (considerably larger than what you paid for it) to take your apartment. LaLa, who can spend $40,000 on a Hermès handbag without batting an eye, just sighed, *Move my entire family for that? I don't think so.* She wasn't going to relocate her family unless the number was even higher. After all the work it took to get Professor N up to the offer we had, the broker got mad at me when LaLa wouldn't accept it. LaLa, her family, her priceless collection of vintage typewriters, and her pet dog Snoopy weren't going to budge. At least I gave it my all.

Now, Professor Niekehle was standing right in front of me ordering a milkshake. *Strawberry? Interesting choice.* After I got my cookies and cream, I looked toward Professor N, and his eyes met mine. I wasn't sure he recognized me, so I approached him. "Hi. I'm Ryan Serhant, the broker for the apartment you wanted to buy."

He took a loud slurp of his milkshake and shrugged like, *Yeah, so?* It was clear he wasn't exactly excited to see me, so I told him to have a great vacation and that it was nice meeting him, and I walked toward the go-cart to begin our treacherous ride back to the hotel on a dirt road in the pitch black of night. Professor N followed me. "It's too much money."

I stopped walking. I knew a few things: (a) Professor N is richer than Midas; (b) it's not about the extra $5 million, it's about *winning*; and (c) if there was another apartment he liked as much as my client's, he would have bought it already because he could buy anything he wanted. I mean, why not just buy the Carlyle Hotel? I turned around, hoping I didn't have any rainbow sprinkles on my face. "My client is happy living where she lives, and she gave you the number it would take to move her entire family."

Professor N nodded and walked off into the island breeze with his bright pink milkshake in tow. Emilia, who has a sixth sense sometimes, watched him walking away. "Ryan, I think he's going to buy that apartment."

I got back to the city, and Professor N's broker called to say he was willing to up his offer. There was much more back-and-forth, and I was given a higher number, but it still wasn't the EXACT number that would get LaLa excited to pack up and move into a new apartment. But I *knew* it was a good number. A record-shattering number. LaLa could wallpaper her new apartment entirely with money if she would just accept this offer.

CRASH!!

That was the sound of a record breaking to bits after I did EVERYTHING IN MY POWER to convince LaLa to accept this enormous amount of money (it wasn't easy). SERHANT. had just broken a record selling an apartment that wasn't even for sale.*

---

* We eventually closed at $48 million.

309

So many factors went into this deal, and I know it would never have happened without the strong foundation of my personal brand. Sure, I had been honing my skills for years, but I knew this sale went beyond being a good negotiator and a hard worker. I wasn't just a random guy selling real estate anymore. I was the face of a carefully curated brand, known for buying and selling luxury real estate all over the world. I had the right experience, connections, work ethic, and confidence, but my brand placed me front and center as The Person who can close high-level and complicated deals. My brand vision also played an important role in this sale. My vision to be the best luxury real estate broker in the world prompted me to challenge myself. *Ryan, can you really make this happen?* When the going got tough, I'd think, *Wait a minute, you're not going to give up, are you? Figure out how to convince the chocolate heiress that this deal is WELL WORTH GRABBING ON TO.* Throughout this entire deal, my brand vision was like a quiet but constant whisper that never let up. It prompted me to keep moving forward, seeking out new solutions, and remembering that I'm not just selling people what they need; I'm showing people what they want. That deal was transformative for me. It showed me that my brand had the power to move mountains—that I could create a greater level of change than I had as just *Ryan Serhant, broker.*

THE BIG MOMENTS

There are many transformative moments that take place during a branding journey. These are the natural result of making significant changes and pushing ourselves past what we all *believe* we can do. These big moments can shed light on new opportunities and clear obstacles on the pathway to success, but you need to be able to recognize them when they land in front of you. As we get ready to wrap up the work we've done together throughout this book, let's look at some of the transformative moments from some of the biggest brands.

KNOW YOUR BRAND . . . REALLY, REALLY KNOW YOUR BRAND!

While living and breathing your brand while you're building it helps get the work done, it is important not to lose perspective, like Tom Bilyeu admits he did: "I learned a really powerful lesson at Quest Nutrition, which is that the way people who found the company think about the company is not often the way the consumer thinks about the brand. We saw Quest as this company we built with grit, determination, hardcore attitude, growth spirit, and warrior mindset. So, we decided to come out with this line of clothing. It wasn't even gym wear—it was almost high-end clothing, like something you'd find at Hugo Boss (but not a suit). Nice stuff. The audience was like, *Bro, do you think I want to buy my high-end clothing from Quaker Oats?* That's how they thought of us . . . as a protein bar, and we were aghast! For us the brand is so much more than a product, but that wasn't coming across in the marketing. You want to be very clear about what your brand is. You want to be very clear about what your brand is not. You want to be clear about who your brand is for and not for. All of those things are very important, but with one goal in mind. Make your audience feel like the company is a person."

THE FEELING YOUR BRAND CONVEYS DOES NOT STOP WITH YOUR PRODUCT OR SERVICE

The experience your customers have with your brand needs to be high quality and consistent, but it also makes sense to think about how noncustomers experience the brand. Mike Evans wanted the positive experience GrubHub provides to extend beyond the people who are using the service to order spring rolls and pad thai: "The brand and the product are a subset of the larger thing I was thinking about, which is . . . experience. Brand is a lot more than what you're advertising and marketing—it's the entire feel of what it's like to interact with the company. Our hiring process is the perfect example. Anyone who came to the office, even if they didn't get the job, got a gift card. We're foodies, and at our core we're a hospitality company. Being hospitable to people who came into the office was a big part of that, and it worked out great. There were times when a candidate didn't get a job, but received a gift card, and would end up referring someone else who was the right match. Rejected candidates became our advocates, and that's because we were trying to create a positive, consistent, hospitable experience across every interaction, not just with customers."

PASSION REALLY MATTERS

The level of work it takes to build a successful brand requires tenacity. Lewis Morgan found passion fueled him during the low moments of building Gym Shark: "Passion obviously plays a key, because you'll go in the trenches. It is very hard to be in the trenches when you aren't making any money. But if you're passionate, you will stay in the trenches, and you will want to make it work."

Daniella Monet also credits her passion for plant-based living with keeping her going: "Obviously, you need to see that there is potential for success, and you need to believe in what you're doing. But I wholeheartedly think if you really believe in something and you're not willing to see it fail, then it won't."

YOU WILL MAKE MISTAKES

Experimenting and expanding will result in mistakes, and that's okay. Griffin Thall thought bikinis were a natural product expansion for his free-living and beachy brand: "We tested bikinis a long time ago, because you'd think, *Oh, bracelets, bikinis! Everyone that wants a bracelet will want a bikini.* As two male business owners, we did not know how specific bikini buying was. Trying to create a bikini brand when we were never going to wear a bikini in our lives (thankfully) wasn't the right move. One Black Friday I said, 'Get these things off our website. We're done with bikinis.' It didn't work. You could call that a failed attempt at product expansion."

ASK FOR THE MOON

Starting any new venture means making mistakes, feeling unsure, and being thirsty for information. Athena Calderone made it her mission to ask people who had more experience than she did: "When I was starting out, I asked so many questions. I would reach out to people who were doing something similar and ask them how they did it. I took so many risks. I don't know who the hell I thought I was, but I asked the famous chef Jean-George, 'Can I come cook in the kitchen at your restaurant ABC and take photos?' Sometimes you might get a door slammed in your face, but so what? Put it out there and ask. Ask for the moon and see where things land. Ask people that have a higher following than you or have paved the way to teach you— or to just get on a call with you. DM people! Just go for it! Ask who can help you. Ask for help when you need it!"

GOODBYE, CAREERS. HELLO, BRANDS.

The era of the "career" is coming to an end. None of us need to jump on the occupation bandwagon, holding on for dear life, riding out all the bumps until we reach some predetermined end of our journey with a sigh of relief. Now we have the power to chart the course on our own terms, and there is no limit to how far we can travel or how much we can experience along the way. But to have the most exciting, lucrative, and satisfying ride, we need to be armed with the power of a personal brand. A brand is your map and compass all in one. Your brand is like a map in that it helps you make the right choices about which roads to take and which ones to avoid at all costs. Your brand is like a compass in that it makes sure you don't stray too far from your desired course as you explore, carving out your own side streets along the way. You will get lost, occasionally wandering too far away from your core, but a solid brand will always guide you back to where you need to be—so there's no need to be afraid.

Whereas a career was a set of rigid expectations, a personal brand is the freedom to build a satisfying life with work you feel passionate about on your own terms. You don't need to burn anything down to do this. I am not telling you to make a radical change, to quit your job, switch industries, start completely fresh. What I am asking you to do is to be open to transformation. Allow yourself to experience all the good that happens when you shift your focus from a "career," and all the old-time ideas that go along with that, to a life built by you and filled with meaningful, satisfying work. That transformation can begin today, and it will be powerful, so get started. There's an entirely new you waiting to be revealed. Put in the work, learn about who you really are, dig deep, and show the world everything your brand has to offer.

As I stand on the highest terrace in the world after a great dinner celebrating the start of another sold-out SellItLikeSerhant.com Mastermind summit, I am still amazed by how far I can see from this jewel in the sky. The lights of Manhattan are spread out below me like a beacon . . . a visual reminder that the city I now call home is bursting with opportunities, new ideas, and potential successes. But from where I'm standing, 1,400 feet above the city, I can see something else. I can see beyond the city . . . the lights slowly fading away to where highways, roads, and bridges branch out to more towns, villages, communities, neighborhoods, and cities. Standing by myself on that terrace, I realize that where the lights of the city end, more opportunities begin, and my brand gives me the freedom to explore them all. SERHANT. isn't beholden to anyone else's rules or expectations, and I can stretch my dreams and goals as far as they can go. It's late, and it's time to head home to Brooklyn, but I take one final look at this breathtaking view of the city where I've put down roots with my family and where my brand was born. The view is spectacular.

While I can't predict what my life will be like a year from now, or what kinds of sales records SERHANT. will have crushed, I do know one thing for sure. The view from wherever I'm standing is bound to be amazing. And now, finally, it's your turn.

When you started this book, you took the first big step in transforming the brand inside of you into something bigger. Whether you knew it or not, that brand was always there, waiting for you to take charge and coax it into something meaningful. You're on the last page of this final chapter and something significant has happened. NOW you have ALL the tools you need to harness the power of your personal brand and use it to scale your business to crazy heights. All that's left for you to do is to put in the work. Are you ready to find the view that inspires you and pushes you to turn that brand inside of you into something huge? I believe you are, and I'm excited to see what you find. Remember, never, ever hold back, because that rookie real estate agent who didn't know what life had in store for him learned one very important lesson . . . there is always more room at the top.

GET READY TO BE TRANSFORMED

READY, SET, GO!

Acknowledgments

Thank you to my wife, Emilia, and our amazing daughter, Zena, for making me the person I am today. Building a personal brand starts with a clear and memorable core identity, and I would not be the wild and crazy emotional roller coaster of a person without you two by my side, every day.

To my parents, my brothers, my sisters, and my long-lost relatives who I meet on 23andMe, thank you for allowing me to once again selfishly use our family name!

To all the agents and staff at SERHANT., our brand is YOU. Thank you for allowing our firm to grow and prosper on the cultural foundation that you all have built.

To Paula Balzer Vitale, the OG AI, the language model before language models, the ChatPBV before the GPT. Thank you for helping me bring the world of Brand It to the masses and helping me complete our Entrepreneur's Trilogy for the betterment of the human race.

To everyone at Hachette for trusting me AGAIN: You have all supported my ideas since our very first meeting, and writing these books has been a huge honor and an unforgettable learning experience. Krishan Trotman, thank you for believing in what I have to say and taking a big chance on a real estate broker.

ACKNOWLEDGMENTS

Lauren Marino, thank you for helping us transform our ideas about branding into a book that will help people everywhere change the course of their lives. Your wisdom, creativity, and patience (especially patience) are greatly appreciated. Michael Barrs, a.k.a "Barrs," you are the best. Thank you for your guidance as we ushered all three books into the world. Mary Ann Naples, thank you for letting me be an author. Working with Hachette is proof positive that getting a degree in English is a perfectly good idea. Thank you to Niyati Patel, Sean Moreau, Allison Gudenau, and Melissa Churchill for getting the job done, and thank you to publicist Michael Giarrantino.

To Brandi Bowles and Natahsa Bolouki at United Talent Agency, Jenn Levy at Netflix, and Randy Barbato, Fenton Bailey, and Breonna Carrerra at World of Wonder. You all believe in me more than I believe in myself!

And to everyone who has ever wanted to start a business or just take that entrepreneurial leap. I know it's scary. But I promise you, on the other side of being afraid is being excited. Step outside of your comfort zone and start something new. That's where the magic is, and I'm looking forward to being your first customer.